A Rhondda Boy

1906 - 1914

IVOR HOWELLS
(seated)

Published in Great Britain 2001

Meadow View
Woodmancote
Elmsworth
Hants. PO10 8RF

Printed by J & P Davison, James Place, Treforest, Pontypridd.

A Rhondda Boy

1906 - 1914

by

Ivor Howells

Published 2001

Foreword

This book was written by Ivor Howells at the age of 93 in a nursing home in Hayling Island in Hampshire. He wrote partly to recapture his memories and in his mind to visit again the Rhondda Valley and his beloved Wales. He also wanted to record the details of life at the beginning of the twentieth century for future generations. After his death at the age of 94 in 1998 a friend and colleague, Owen Vernon Jones, suggested it might be published. Very grateful thanks is owed to him for all the hard work involved in editing and searching out interesting photographs from local sources. It is due to his invaluable help and encouragement that this book now appears in print. Ivor would have been thrilled and amazed to read the printed version.

Edward Howells

Contents

Editor's Preface

Owen Vernon Jones

Son of a miner, Rhondda born and bred, Rhondda educated apart from his degree years at Aberystwyth, Ivor Howells spent all his professional life as teacher and headmaster in Rhondda schools. After graduating he taught for a short time in Llwyncelyn Elementary School before returning as French master to Porth County School for Boys, his old school. Following a successful headship of Porth Secondary School he was appointed Headmaster of Tonypandy Secondary School. Thus in breadth of experience of Rhondda grammar schools he may claim to be without rival. Over a span of forty years in the profession he would be known to thousands of boys and girls.

A delicate, studious, sensitive and observant boy he retained a remarkable, clear graphic memory when he penned his memoirs at the age of ninety-three. His original account ranges from the first decade of the century to the forties but it has been decided for practical reasons to limit the present publication to his Porth boyhood and primary school period. Indeed his recollections are material enough for at least one further book. He wrote as he remembered with asides and often detailed description here limited.

We are forcibly returned, as we should be, to Porth before the petrol engine, in the age of coal and steam, to difficult and dangerous times when the mass of the male population, man and boy, were prisoners of the pit. The sole escape for a fortunate few was via education. He does not paint a pretty picture and certainly does not bathe in a warm glow of nostalgia remembering only what was best, ‘the false memory syndrome’. Yet he was impelled to recall and record. He attempts to explain the apparent contradiction in terms of 'hiraeth', ' a word with more than one meaning in Welsh and no exact equivalent in English'. It has been taken by Matthew Arnold as a characteristic of the Celts in general.

His setting is Porth where both valleys meet, typical of Rhondda. His elementary school was at Cymmer when Dan Jones was headmaster. A school had been opened there in 1859 by the Anglican National Society. Forster's Act provided for such schools by law in 1870. In 1881 a new school was opened with three departments and T. T. Davies was Head of the boys' school. He continued in this capacity to the age of seventy six! Dan Jones was appointed to a co-headship with him and retired in 1926, having been sole Head since 1895.

Dan Jones gives his own impressive account of early Porth in a couple of scholarly articles for 'The Official Souvenir Programme for Porth's Empire Shopping Week' of March 1931. The name 'Cymmer', he says, was used for the whole district now known as 'Porth', deriving from 'Cymmer fi', 'Take me'. It indicates that two rivers of the same name met there. With the development of the Taff Vale Railway and of the collieries, 'Porth' was increasingly used, signifying entrance or gateway to the two valleys. The title of his article and the cover of the programme are a proud assertion, using a different image, of the aptness of the name, 'Porth, the Hub of the Rhondda'.

There seems to be little doubt that Porth owed much to this commanding position. In addition to its elementary schools it had a Pupil Teacher Centre, the Cambrian Mining School, the Commercial School, the South Wales Bible Institute, Porth Secondary School, the Rhondda Intermediate School. It had a hospital, a park and was the centre of William Evans’ nationwide business empire. Porth and pop went together like Rhondda and coal.

I knew Ivor well as a member of staff at Porth County when his son Dr. Edward (Lynn) Howells was a pupil and later when he was Headmaster of Tonypandy Secondary School and I was Head of Porth County.

Bachgen o'r Rhondda oedd Ivor Howells. Yn ei lyfr mae e'n rhoi i ni darlun o fywyd yn y Rhondda ar ddechrau'r ganrif. Bywyd caled roedd hwnnw.

Mae Ivor Howells wedi ysgrifennu mewn ffordd syml, hawdd ei ddarllen. Mae e'n disgrifio pobl Porth, eu harferion a'r digwyddiadau fel trwy lygaid plentyn. Mae'r bobl yn bobl cyffredin, ond maen nhw'n bwysig fel cymeriadau mewn cymuned fach. Maen nhw'n haeddu gael eu cofio achos maen nhw'n dangos pa fath o gymeriadau oedd yn byw ym Mhorth ar y pryd. Mae llawer o bobl wedi dweud bod cymeriadau'r Rhondda yn y gorffenol yn wahanol ac yn aml yn cael eu hadnabod trwy eu llysenwau. Mae Ivor Howells wedi rhoi i ni darlun o'u byd wrth ddisgrifio'r amser pan oedd e'n fachgen ym Mhorth.

Porth Secondary School football team 1948-49

Porth Secondary: teachers at the school in 1953. Ivor Howells centre seated.

Hiraeth

The word 'hiraeth' is untranslatable. There is no word in English to express its meaning. It sums up the intense longing of every Welshman to return to his native land. But, strangely enough, when opportunity presents itself, he does not do so! How can one explain this contradiction? The answer may be found in our history. The short answer is coal! The word 'Rhondda' was once synonymous with the word 'coal' and every lump of coal had blood on it! One does not come back to relive our horrendous history and troublesome times. Yet the pull persists and we can't forget.

Who can forget the picture of a retired miner in the last stages of emphysema gasping for breath, his lungs filled with coal dust, or the miner whose eyes are permanently affected by nystagmus brought on by working for years in semi darkness? Who can forget the pit ponies condemned for life to darkness and danger, pulling heavy trams filled with coal along treacherous surfaces. Even the aid of the tiny canary was enlisted, used to detect the presence of that deadly enemy called 'gas' long before it became apparent to the men. It displayed signs of distress, thereby giving warning that danger was lurking in the darkness unseen. Many lives were thus saved.

Who can forget the thoughtless greed of coal owners who took the easy way of getting rid of colliery waste by depositing it along the mountainside? This practice was continued even after the mines were nationalised in 1947 with the inevitable result of the Aberfan disaster in 1966 when a tip, sodden and heavy after weeks of continuous rain, suddenly slipped down the mountain side and engulfed a school causing a horrible and sudden death to over a hundred human beings, teachers and pupils alike. The mines have all been closed, steps have been taken to remove these tips scattered all over the mining valleys, but they had been left for so long to offend the eyes of valley people, monuments to man's greed. They were not completely eradicated until mercifully, nature gradually took over to bury these monstrosities from sight forever.

Even the river was subjected to a daily intake of colliery waste and what was once a sparkling trout-filled stream was transformed into a slowly moving mass of black sludge.

How many times did the housewife have to take in the washing from the outside clothes line to be rewashed because a wind blowing in the wrong direction had deposited on the clothes a film of coal dust! Imagine the fear and anguish of the miners' wives when at five thirty in the morning, they prepared their men for their arduous and dangerous work; as they filled the "Tommy boxes" with bread and cheese and the "jacks" with water or cold tea – no thermos flasks in those days – for their mid-shift meal, wondering as the men left the house for the seven a.m. shift whether they would see them alive again.

All day long, they would listen for that dreaded sound, the frantic wail of the colliery hooter which would indicate an accident, a roof fall or, worse still, most feared of all, an explosion. Women would rush to the pithead, often with a baby in arms and toddler at their feet. They would watch the rescue squad, brave men all and specially trained, arrive with rescue apparatus and the inevitable canary, who would descend the mine not knowing what dangers they would meet but bravely willing to risk all to succour their mates. Sometimes they would emerge from the cage; their faces covered with dust and sweat, bearing a stretcher carrying an injured or even a dead miner.

An explosion was caused by a collection of methane gas, called firedamp. After an explosion came the poisonous carbon monoxide gas, which killed without warning. There was no escape! They all died instantly! There were sometimes hundreds of casualties and the bodies were found in the position of eating their food or cutting coal. Death was swift and sudden!

I remember the explosion of 1913 at Senghenydd, a small mining village in an adjoining valley when over 400 men died, almost the whole of the adult male population. As I walked through the main street with my father, there was no one to be seen, not a sound to be heard. It was a village of the dead! It was a scene never to be forgotten.

At this terrible scene, a wave of fear swept over my heart and I searched for my father's hand, and he, understanding, patted me reassuringly on the head. We trudged our way home, not a word was said, but unspoken questions filled our minds. Was coal worth this death and desolation? Would the scars in the hearts of these stricken souls ever be healed?

Another hazard faced by the miners was floods, fortunately, very rare happenings. In 1877 the Tynewydd pit about a mile from my home suffered heavy flooding. Fortunately too, ample warning was given and most of the miners were speedily evacuated except for four men and a boy, who were forced to retreat before the advancing flood, until they were trapped at a dead end and could retreat no further. The pocket in which they found themselves was so small that the air became compressed so that it presented a wall of resistance against the flood. There, the water stood like a wild beast, deprived of its prey and ready to pounce when opportunity presented itself.

There they lived or, rather, existed for five long days in complete darkness, their oil lamps having long failed. They had no food or water, having left their jacks and Tommy boxes behind in their rush to escape the flood. They spent much of the time praying and singing hymns to keep up their spirits. The singing helped break the silence of their tiny cave, a silence broken only by ominous creaking in the roof above, threatening at any moment to bring down a heavy fall. Now and again, they would fall into uneasy sleep to awake to stark reality. Would the waters finally break through and bring their lives to a speedy end? Or would they succumb, one by one, to a slow and lingering death?

But relief was at hand. They were heartened to hear the efforts of rescuers as they hacked at the obdurate rock surface to get through to them. These brave men worked unremittingly for 5 whole days, shifts following each other in quick succession as men fell back in sheer exhaustion. The work was hard; all done by hand in those days. At last, they were through! The entombed men were rescued, literally snatched from the jaws of death! One can imagine the sense of relief, the cries of joy and jubilation of the general public when the news broke through to them. The men were treated as the heroes they were. The entombment of these men and their subsequent rescue, rank as an epic event in the annals of the Welsh coal field.

One of the men, David Jenkins (Dafydd Siencyn) never went down the mines again and later in life kept a greengrocer's shop. When trade was slack and customers few, he could be seen outside his shop, white-whiskered, wearing a broad-brimmed Quaker-like black hat, puffing away contentedly at his clay pipe. I often saw him on my way to and from school. I looked upon him in awe and often wondered where his thoughts were.

Strikes broke out at irregular intervals like 'flu epidemics. The strike of 1910, the famous Tonypandy Riots, witnessed violent scenes. The miners, incensed by failure of negotiations, ran riot through the main street of Tonypandy, breaking windows and looting shops, to be repelled by violent baton charges of the police who wielded their weapons to such effect that there were many sore heads in the miners' homes the following morning. The strike left a bitter legacy. The Tonypandy Riots lingered long in the memory. At the age of six I was too young to know the reason for the strike or its outcome.

I have, also, very vague recollections of the 1921 strike, during my last year at school endeavouring to win enough scholarships to fund me through university. I worked very hard doing five hours' work every night from five to ten o'clock after school. There were no grants in those days! It was a glorious summer with sunshine throughout of which the miners took full advantage spending many happy hours in the open air. It was a pleasure to see the pit ponies, brought up for the duration of the strike, as they galloped around the fields in gay abandon, throwing themselves on the ground and kicking their legs about in mad ecstasy as they revelled in the unfamiliar green meadow and succulent grass. A squad of soldiers brought in to quell any possible disturbance fraternised amicably with the locals, especially the female section. All was peace and quiet! The strike lingered on for some months and my recollection is that it ended indecisively.

The 1926 strike was a different affair. It happened at the end of the first year of my teaching career. It began as a general strike with all the Unions taking part. But the other Unions soon withdrew, leaving the miners to battle alone. Perhaps with hindsight, it would have been better if they had continued to negotiate, but they were led by a maverick leader called A.J. Cook, a native of my town who lived quite near. His fiery eloquence and battlecry of "Not a penny off the pay, not a minute on the day" and the loyalty of the miners kept the strike going for six months.

As the summer ended and merged into dismal autumn, the distress of the miners was clearly to be seen. Money was short and food scarce. My father was a miner, and it was only my salary, which kept the family going. The only breadwinner, I gave up my whole salary every month, keeping only ten shillings for personal expenses. The authorities had to open feeding centres, commonly called 'soup kitchens', in the schools. If the accommodation at the schools was inadequate, they were opened in the vestries of the local chapels. There the miners' children were fed with what was in many cases the only substantial meal of the day. The cooperation of the public was magnificent. Everyone rallied round, money collections were made and gifts of clothes and food generously given and readily received. The schoolteachers gave up part of their holidays to supervise the children at the feeding centres – no demand for extra pay for extra responsibilities in those days.

And so the strike went on and here the ingenuity and resourcefulness of the miners took a hand. This was the time of the famous 'jazz bands'. Their musical instruments called 'gazookas', known also as Kazoos, were somewhat akin to the paper and comb instruments, which the children used to use. Bands of cowboys, Red Indians, Sheikhs of Araby, Pierrots, clowns, soldiers and sailors were formed with their uniforms correct to the last detail. It was incredible! How they managed it I shall never know! They spent hours marching and counter-marching in all kinds of bewildering formations until they were perfect. A Guards regiment would have been proud of them. They learned and tootled marching songs and marched with verve. Competitions between the bands were held on various football fields and prizes given. They sometimes practised their marching through the streets of the town, and everyone left what they were doing to watch. Collections were made during the march, and the proceeds given to the miners' distress fund. Everyone gave generously. Competitions became so popular that they were continued long after the strike ended.

But as autumn merged into winter and the cold weather began, spirits drooped, enthusiasm waned, and the miners grew weary. As Christmas drew near, they gave in. Negotiations took place, agreement was reached, and they went back to work. It was abject defeat! They went back worse off then when they started. Wages were cut, hundreds of men were dismissed, and a half-hour added to the working day. My father was one of those dismissed and at the early age of fifty-two, never worked again. The trials and tribulations of the strike were never forgotten and left bitterness in the hearts of the miners. It was indeed a very dismal Christmas that followed!

Gradually, the financial situation improved, but the menacing shadow of Hitler was slowly, but surely, appearing on the horizon, largely ignored by the British people.

The 'hiraeth', the old longing, the feeling for those of the past, is there and motivates these reminiscences but the native does not return except in memory.

My Early Days

My Ancestors, Called From Country by Coal

I can go no further back in my ancestry than my four grandparents, who were all alive when I came on the scene. They played an important role in my early life.

The names of my maternal grandparents were John Richard Jones and Mary Jones. They came to the Rhondda Valley from a little hamlet called Penrhyn Coch situated on the bare uplands of North Cardiganshire about eight miles from Aberystwyth. My grandfather was a farm labourer eking a meagre living on the hills, lured to the Rhondda by the prospect of far better wages amongst the coalmines. My grandmother, as far as I can ascertain, was a servant in a nearby mansion house called Nant-yr-Eos (nightingale's brook). My grandfather was a fluent Welsh speaker, but my grandmother came originally from South Pembrokeshire, which was largely anglicised by the influx of a band of Flemish weavers who many years before were forced to escape from religious persecution in their native land and settled down in that part of the country which became known as "Little England beyond Wales". My grandmother's Welsh was consequently halting with a strange accent.

They came to the Rhondda about 1885 when my mother was three or four years old. They settled in what was called a company house, built and owned by the Colliery Company, Messrs Insole Ltd. It was a tiny cottage with no garden at 84 High Street, Cymmer. They later moved to a slightly larger house with a sizeable garden at 164 High Street.

They had four children, my mother, Maria born on 15th June 1882, Elisabeth Ann (Nannie), Martha Jane and much later, on the 4th July 1899, Thomas John (Tommy John and later, Tom). My grandparents were a comely couple and all their children had good looks. Tom was six feet in height, considered to be very tall in those days. My grandfather was a nice man, gentle in manner and quietly spoken. I was very fond of him. He must have been intelligent, for he attained the position of an official called a fireman, which entailed the passing of a rigorous written examination. He was in charge of a district in the mine and was responsible for the safety of the men in his charge. My grandmother was a good housewife, and the house was always spotlessly clean. Grandfather earned a good wage, and they always seemed comfortably off. They were a happy family.

My paternal grandparents had already retired to Ferryside, their place of birth, before I came into the world. Ferryside was a sizeable village situated at the estuary of the River Towy, a noted salmon River. My grandfather was rather unprepossessing in appearance with narrow shoulders, small blinking eyes and straggly, white whiskers. His name was Thomas William. My grandmother, Hannah by name, was stoutly built and plain featured. My grandfather must have been financially a shrewd man because when he retired, he was the owner of 4 cottages, the rent of which provided him with a comfortable living. This was supplemented by the State provision of ten shillings a week introduced by Mr Lloyd George in 1910. They had two children; Eleanor born in 1874 and my father, who was born on 12th January 1876 and named William. I must confess that I was not over fond of them and preferred my maternal grandparents.

My father married my mother in 1899, and they had eight children; William John (Willie John, later Bill) born December 12th 1899, Thomas Clifford, born 1902 who died at three months, myself born 4th June 1904, Oliver born 1906 who died at 2 months, Lena May born 30th January 1908, Hannah Mary (named after both grandparents, but called Nana) born March 2nd 1912, Trevor born 16th December 1913 and a baby born prematurely on 23rd May 1918. My mother died giving birth to the last baby, cause of death – kidney failure.

I was born on a beautifully warm sunny day, sooner than expected for my mother was busy preparing to spend the afternoon at the visiting fun fair in the town when arrangements had to be cancelled. I was a sickly child, having caught pneumonia when I was only three weeks old. Pneumonia in those days was a serious illness causing many deaths. The age of antibiotics was far distant, and one had to depend on one's constitution to combat the disease. Superstition and old wives' tales were rife. My father was told that if one obtained a pair of sheep's lungs and placed them at the feet of the patient for a few days, he would recover. Accordingly, my father went to the local slaughterhouse (not called 'abattoir' in those days), obtained them and placed them at my feet as instructed. The normal course of this disease was that on the nineth day 'the crisis' occurred, at the end of which the patient either started to sweat profusely, sending the body temperature falling rapidly like a stone, and recovered - or the lungs filled with fluid, and he died. I was lucky and survived, much to the amazement of the local doctor who had given up all hope of recovery. He told my mother, "Marvellous! Watch him! He is going to go far. He's got the will to live". And perhaps as I am now 94 years old when writing these words, he was not far wrong. Sometimes I wonder whether my father thought it was the sheep's lungs, which had really saved me.

The illness left its mark on me. I suffered with bronchial trouble, especially in winter, and was short of breath with a constantly wheezing chest. Matters came to a head when the doctor informed my parents that unless they moved me from the coal dust of the valleys he could not guarantee a healthy life or even survival.

Accordingly, after much heart searching, it was decided that I should spend the whole of the next summer months with my grandparents at Ferryside I was then four years old. I did not look forward to going for I stood in some awe of my grandparents, who were not outwardly very affectionate. However my fears were unfounded as they proved to be very kind and did their utmost to make me happy and comfortable. I was very grateful. That visit was a revelation and a turning point in my life. A New World was offered to me.

A Summer in Ferryside 1908

A return to the rural past

Ferryside is a pretty village situated on the estuary of the River Towy. On the other side of the estuary is the village of Llanstephan (Stephen's Church), dominated by the ruins of an old Norman castle on the summit of the hill behind. Further west, but perfectly visible, is the estuary of the River Taf, a trout river on which stood the village of Laugharne. Dylan Thomas lived here for some years in his house called 'The Boathouse' where he wrote some of his poems. He would stagger home uproariously drunk to his quick-tempered wife Caitlin, with whom he had a quarrel wracked tempestuous relationship.

At Ferryside, the tide ebbed far and fast, leaving a vast expanse of golden sand which housed fertile cockle beds. Sometimes my grandfather would gather a bucketful of cockles, which we ate for our afternoon tea. They were boiled in a saucepan and, the water having been drawn, they were put steaming hot in a huge tureen, placed in the centre of the table, from which we helped ourselves as we wished, accompanied by a crusty, homemade bread and creamy country butter. It was only later in life that I realised that we had been guilty of boiling alive hundreds of living creatures! Prior to this revelation I thought in my innocence that they were simply objects found in the sand. I never ate any more cockles after that discovery, but they were certainly delicious. The cockle shells were thrown on the garden path where they provided a firm, if noisy, foundation.

There were professional cockle gatherers, mostly women who lived in a little village called Llansaint about two miles from Ferryside and appropriately called the 'Cockle Village' (the birthplace of Gerald Davies, the famous international rugby player). They had to be careful at low tide as the sea came in, as quickly as it went out and there was always the danger of being cut off. They came warmly clad, accompanied by donkeys carrying sacks and riddles. The cockles were gathered in the sacks which they took to the nearby railway station where they were weighed, labelled, and despatched by the next train to Swansea to be sold in the local market. They were a great favourite with the local folk. It was an arduous occupation as it entailed standing or crouching for hours, often in bitter winds. The poor donkeys had to endure these conditions.

Near the beach stood the lifeboat house with a stone tablet on the outside wall stating the number of times the lifeboat had been called out, the dates, the name of the ship and the number of lives saved. It was thrilling to see the lifeboat men at their practice drills, and I was amazed to see the speed at which they launched the boat. At low tide, the remains of a wrecked ship called the *Old Paul* were plainly visible.

Ferryside is on the main railway line of Fishguard to Paddington. The station was scrupulously clean; litter free and decorated by numerous pots of pretty flowers in the summer. Sometimes I would sit with my grandfather on a seat on the platform and watch with wonder and some fear as the express trains came speeding past, whistles screaming frantically, rushing through with a deafening roar which shook the station to its very foundations. When the local trains stopped to disgorge its passengers, I would gaze with wonder and admiration at the engine, a steaming monster that seemed resentful at being stopped and only too ready to take flight again. Once I was allowed to stay up from bed to see the 8.20 p.m. mail train. The mailbag was placed on a lofty gantry and as the train roared past, it snatched the bag from its perch without stopping or even slowing down, a sight, which remained in my memory.

Once a week we would go down to the beach to see the fishermen landing their catch, which consisted mainly of a fish called 'flat fish', which was really plaice. We would purchase a few pounds, which we would enjoy at lunch the following day.

My grandfather kept a large vegetable garden – no flowers, as you can't eat flowers – in front of the house where I would play happily for hours and whose produce proved very tasty at the lunch of the day.

My grandmother had cousins who kept two farms in the near vicinity. One was called Robert's Rest – I had no idea who Robert was and nor did anyone else! He must have lived a long time ago.

The other was Tycanol (middle house), and we often went there on visits. I would see the cows being milked by hand in the yard in front of the house, a task I thought very tedious. I thought them huge, stupid looking, lumbering beasts and I was a little afraid of them. I would be given a glass of warm foaming milk straight from the cow – no pasteurisation in those days - or a glass of buttermilk, which I found very rich. The milk would be taken to a dairy with thick stone walls to keep it cool. There on stone shelves and tables I would see huge shallow vats with milk slowly curdling into butter.

Sometimes my grandmother would take me for a ride in the country in a governess cart which she drove herself. She would give the little pony no respite for she kept on shaking the reins or clicking her tongue, urging him to go faster. He would respond by going at a slow reluctant trot on the outward journey, which developed into a smart canter on the way back. He knew only too well that he was on his way home to a warm, comfortable stable, a well-deserved rest and a feed of sweet smelling hay.

Sometimes, my grandfather would take me for country walks eastwards along the coastal road as far as an old church, St. Ishmael, passing on the way a noted landmark called Big Ben, a huge rocky promontory permanently half submerged in the sea. Or we would go westwards to a little hamlet called Cwm Mill, near which was a large mansion house, Iscoed, which was the former residence of General Picton, who was killed in The Battle of Waterloo. On the way my grandfather would often pick herbs from the hedgerows and eat them. One day I ate a dandelion leaf, which I promptly spat out as it had a burning taste. My grandfather, who rarely smiled, laughed heartily at my discomfiture much to my annoyance.

My bedroom looked westwards, and when I had finished my supper of biscuits and a glass of milk; I retired to the bedroom, which had a clean country smell, with its cool white sheets. On a sunny evening the sunsets were magnificent. The vivid red and blue colours of the early evening would yield to the more delicate pastel shades of green with pink and yellow of the setting sun as it reluctantly sank behind the ruins of Llanstephan Castle on the opposite coast of the estuary. I was entranced as it cast a golden glow along the western horizon. When the light finally sank from view, I would lie contentedly, pleasantly tired after the labours of the day, finally drifting into a deep, dreamless sleep. It was heaven!

Although Ferryside was a small village, there were great differences socially and economically among the inhabitants. In an obscure corner of the village, almost hidden from sight, was a tiny quarter called 'The Back and Bully'. It was not a very salubrious area, and my grandmother warned me not to go near unless accompanied. However I caught fleeting glimpses as I passed that way. The inhabitants were people in strained circumstances, aged couples living on the meagre State pension of ten shillings a week, elderly widows, the workshy and men engaged in intermittent employment. The cottages were small with tiny windows and dim interiors. There was an unkempt air about the whole place with an allpervading smell of fish and cockles.

In one of these cottages lived my grandmother's brother William, called W for some reason. One day when we arrived, he was smoking a clay pipe with a long stem which gave out clouds of pungent smoke that hung around the corners of the room and eventually pervaded the whole atmosphere. The room itself was disorderly and sparsely furnished. When my grandmother started talking to him in Welsh, apparently upraiding him on his way of life, he said nothing except to utter sundry grunts accompanied by cries of dissent in defence from his equally slatternly wife. At last my grandmother, realising that she was making no headway, went into a huff and clutching my hand, swept hurriedly out of the room, uttering a loud, contemptuous snort as she slammed the door on the way out. He certainly was a disreputable character living in disreputable surroundings. He evidently was the 'black sheep' of the family.

In the centre of the village were better class, bigger, villa-like houses with extensive well kept gardens which housed white collar workers, clerks and shop assistants who travelled by train to Carmarthen about 8 miles distant. The village itself was situated at the foot of a steep slope called 'The Cliff', at the summit of which lay an extensive plateau where stood the mansion houses of the county families like the Brigstocks or industrial magnates like the Nevilles. They were imposing residences with extensive lawns, beautiful flowerbeds and long winding drives. The industrialists were owners or directors of the tinplate works at Llanelli or the copper works at Swansea, to which they travelled daily by train (no motor cars yet).

Passing one day, I noticed that where one of the lawns was set apart two white posts had been erected with a net extended between them and there was to be seen four wraithlike figures in white, hitting a small white ball to each other. This was my first introduction to the game of tennis. At that time I thought it a rather futile exercise as I saw no purpose in one pair returning the ball as if they did not want it and less purpose still when they failed to return it and they started all over again. My interest quickly waned, and I soon wandered off.

One Saturday morning my grandfather took me to the cattle market at Carmarthen. On the way in we saw a number of farmers sitting on benches outside a public house quaffing huge tankards of foaming beer. They were dressed either in breeches and leggings or in rough tweed suits with cloth caps or trilby hats on their heads. Some of them, removing their headgear in the warm morning sunshine, revealed faces of astonishing contrast, the lower part being brown and weather beaten with the upper white and pale pink. This was a strange sight to someone accustomed to the miners' pallid faces.

We reached the market. It was Bedlam! It was pandemonium! It was a scene, which defied description. The snuffling grunts of the pigs, the neighing of the horses, the crowing of the cockerels, the bleating of the sheep, the lowing of the cows and the bellowing of the bulls produced a cacophony of sound. The noise deafened the ears while the pervading animal smells assailing our nostrils made it difficult to breathe. In one corner was the auction ring, where one could hear the monotonous patter of the auctioneer urging the hardheaded farmers to increase their bids. In another corner was the cheapjack cajoling onlookers with his cheerful chatter to start the bidding. The prospective buyers, who had seen it all before, waited expectantly until he reduced his prices, which he inevitably and ultimately did. He pretended all the while that he was practically giving his goods away and that they were making him a pauper. Probably he was making a handsome profit. To me, it was like an unhappy nightmare peopled by noisy animals and mad human beings. It was too much! Clutching my grandfather's hand, I escaped this scene of horror, much to his amusement.

My grandmother had a niece who worked as a parlour maid at one of the mansion houses. On one of her visits she suggested that it would be a good idea if I could come to the house and play with the young son, 3 years of age, whose name was Tony. The parents' consent was sought and they readily agreed, so I went. It was a revelation! The house was beautiful, with countless large rooms with high lofty ceilings, tastefully furnished, walls beautifully decorated and hung with large magnificent pictures of sea and country. I was entranced! as I gazed openmouthed at all this beauty.

Tony had a nanny and spent most of his time in a room called 'the nursery'. There or in the grounds we played together and we agreed so well that my visits became a permanent feature. I spent every day there during the rest of my stay at Ferryside. His toys were outstanding and entirely new to me. We had lunch together and I thoroughly enjoyed the food. Sometimes, when the weather was fine, we had picnics on the beach and under the watchful eye of the nurse we paddled in the sea and built sandcastles to our hearts content. We had supper at 6 o'clock, and then Tony was washed, taken to the drawing room and presented to his parents, to whom he related the events of the day. His parents took to me kindly and often laughed at what they termed my quaint sayings. When Tony was put to bed, my grandmother's niece took me home.

So the days sped by, and the day for my departure drew ever nearer. My spirits sank lower and lower. Some days before my departure, my grandmother took me to Miss Thomas' shop, apparently to buy a present for my mother. This shop was a real Aladdin's Cave containing all kinds of untold treasures, and amid the motley collection of articles along the shelves, I espied a box shaped helmet which used to adorn the heads of the members of an organisation called The Boys' Brigade somewhat akin to the Boy Scouts. It took my fancy, and I refused to leave the shop until she bought it for me. I immediately donned it and leaving the shop I proudly marched along the street, to my grandmother's embarrassment.

At last the fateful day of departure arrived, and as I reluctantly boarded the train, I bade a fond farewell to my grandparents who had done so much to make my stay a happy one. As the train left the station and passed all the landmarks, my grandparents' house and garden, Llanstephan Castle on the other side of the estuary, its ruins sharply outlined against the morning sky, the stately mansion houses on the cliff, the golden sands and the sun-kissed wavelets of the blue-grey sea, Big Ben thrusting itself proudly and defiantly into the incoming tide, St Ishmael's church, all landmarks which had become very dear to me – my spirits sank to a low depth of deep despondency.

At last the journey ended and we arrived at Porth station. Great was my father's amazement when he saw a diminutive figure emerge from the train and strut proudly along the platform, marching head erect, like a soldier complete with helmet atop, to the amusement of bystanders. My father made me discard the helmet before we left the station. It was a Saturday afternoon in mid September and after the pure clean air of Ferryside, I found the atmosphere heavy and suffocating. In those days miners did not receive their pay until Saturday afternoon, so that Saturday evening was shopping day. The main street was crowded and shops were allowed to stay open until eleven o'clock. I was now unaccustomed to crowds and as I stood in the dusty street, I made up my mind that as soon as I grew up, I would leave the Rhondda Valley and seek more pleasant pastures. Little did I know that Fate decreed that I should spend my first sixty years amid the coalfields.

An amazing feature of this period of my life is that I cannot remember who accompanied me on my journey to and from Ferryside. Someone must have been my guide and counsellor, for the journey was quite arduous and lasted about four hours necessitating a change of stations from the Rhondda and Swansea Bay railway (R.S.B.R.) to the Great Western Railway (G.W.R.) at a place called Briton Ferry. My memory is completely blank on this matter.

Early Home Life

I lived for the major part of my life in the mining town of Porth in the Rhondda Valley. The town had approximately 20,000 inhabitants in its heyday and was appropriately named because the word 'Porth' means 'an entrance or gateway' and the town stood at the entrance to the Rhondda Valley. There are in fact two Rhondda valleys, the Rhondda Fawr (Big Rhondda) and Rhondda Fach (Little Rhondda), converging to meet at Porth. From there the River Rhondda flows to the town of Pontypridd where it joins the River Taff which flows on to the sea (the Bristol Channel) at Cardiff, the administrative capital of Wales.

Both valleys are extremely narrow, in places ravine like, with room at the bottom only for the river, the road and railway. The sides of the valleys are extremely steep, rising at the highest point to 1100 feet, and along the slopes are row after row of tiny terraced houses, all so alike. They seem to cling to the steep slopes, as if

Hannah Street from 'William Evans' by Owen Vernon Jones

about to fall into the valley below. In both valleys, the villages and townships stand so closely together that it is difficult to determine where one ends and the next begins. It is simply a long line of houses extending on both sides from the top end to the bottom end of the valley with hardly any empty spaces between.

In Porth itself, the river runs through the centre of the town, having on one side the main street, the shopping centre called Hannah Street and on the other, in those days the Cymmer colliery pit head. The pit, from its central position, dominated the whole place and simply refused to be ignored. The area around the town had various districts, close together, but yet distinctly separate. Some of them were peculiarly named, one being called Britannia. Why such a typical Welsh mining district was thus named was always a mystery still unsolved. There was another called America Fach (Little America), so called because its public house bore, for no known reason, the name New York Hotel.

On the utmost outskirts of the town was a district named Mount Pleasant, so called I should imagine, because it was the only area of the town outside the sight and sound of the pit. It contained houses of a better type than the usual miner's cottage. Some were semi detached, and a few detached with tiny lawns in front which we called 'greens'. Here were housed members of the professional classes; colliery officials, bank managers, solicitors, ministers of religion, school teachers and the like.

A steep road to the northeast of the town led to a district called Nyth Bran (Crow's Nest) so named because of its position high on the hill. Another road to the south of the town led steeply through the village of Cymmer, up an ever-increasing gradient reaching 1 : 4 near the summit before it reached the hill village of Trebanog about 700 feet above sea level. From Trebanog, the road ran steeply down to the village of Tonyrefail (the town with a smithy) at the bottom. By traversing this road, one crossed the last range of mountains, which divided the mining valleys from the coastal plain of Glamorgan. Thereafter lay the verdant country of the Vale of Glamorgan and ahead the seaside resorts of Porthcawl, Llantwit Major, Barry and Penarth, washed by the waters of the Bristol Channel.

I lived at No. 3 Blosse Terrace in a street of 11 houses which sloped gently downwards and not far from the bottom of which stood the Cymmer colliery pit head, so we lived within constant sight and sound of coal workings. The first 3 houses, which included our home, were the property of my grandfather. They had been built before the others and there was, consequently, a gap between them, which gave us the luxury of a side entrance, a convenience rarely found in this valley of, terraced houses. This gap was called 'gwli' which, I suppose, was the Welsh version of gully. For this house we paid our grandfather a monthly rent of 13 shillings, a negligible sum in these days, but one to be reckoned with then when we consider that 1s 6d would purchase a return railway ticket to Cardiff, 16 miles away, or a lunch of soup, plaice and chips and a pudding at one of Cardiff's restaurants.

The house consisted of three bedrooms upstairs, together with a small cupboard under the staircase, complete with door, which we called the 'cwtch' and to which our cat always repaired to have her kittens – a regular event. One of the rooms downstairs was the living room which we called the kitchen. The other, called the parlour, was rarely used in the winter because we could not afford to buy the additional coal necessary to light a fire. Attached to the main building was a smaller one-storey building containing the scullery which we called the 'lobby', the pantry and a much smaller room with a separate outside door which was, of course, the lavatory – the word 'toilet' had not yet come into use. The lobby door opened out into the back yard with a side entrance, which contained the coalhouse, called the 'coal cwtch'. Last of all was a fair-sized garden, which was rarely cultivated. My father, no doubt, was too tired after a hard day's labour in the mine to do this additional work.

When we first lived in the house, the water tap was situated in the back yard. This presented us with many problems in the winter as it often froze up and it was very difficult to unfreeze it. Eventually, it was transferred to the lobby, which was a great relief. The floors of the two bedrooms and two main rooms downstairs were covered with linoleum with a few small carpets which we called mats. The lobby floor was simply flag stones covered with a coconut mat. The pantry floor and that of the cwtch were left uncovered but the stairs also had linoleum.

It was considered wise in those days when building houses to locate the lavatory, for obvious reasons, far away from the main building. Indeed, when the earlier houses were built, it was to be found at the far end of the garden, which necessitated a fairly lengthy walk for would-be users and a rather hazardous one at nighttime. Toilet paper was unknown, and people used newspapers. The more discerning cut squares of paper in appropriate sizes, others simply did not bother, but used the paper as required. Some people did not take newspapers and I shudder to think what method they used.

Inside toilets were a thing of the future. If nature called during the night, recourse had to be made to the use of a chamber pot under the bed, giving the poor housewife next morning the unpleasant task of emptying the contents into a bucket to be taken downstairs and flushed away in the outside toilet.

All the rooms were sparsely furnished on purely utilitarian lines. The kitchen had just a table, a few chairs and a sofa. The table was covered with oil cloth – no table cloth. Tablecloths were used only on special occasions, which were few. The fireplace was huge, having on one side the oven, which was the sole means of cooking, and on the other, a hob on which was placed the kettle. The hearthstone had to be washed, cleaned and white-stoned every day and on it stood the fender with fire irons. This also had to be polished every day. All around was a huge fireguard, which covered not only the grate, but also the whole fireplace.

One night, this fireguard nearly caused a great tragedy, which might have cost us our lives. We had retired to bed and I had fallen asleep, when, suddenly, I awoke with a start. I felt there was something-untoward happening – smoke! I could smell smoke? Smoke in a bedroom? Impossible? I wrinkled my nose, unmistakable this time. It was smoke. I opened my eyes and the room was full of smoke. I aroused my brother who was asleep beside me. He lit a candle and, to our horror, we found that what I had suspected was all too true. Panic stations! We rushed to alert my father in the next bedroom and we all tumbled downstairs, opened the kitchen door and the source was plain for all to see. My mother was in the habit of putting my father's working clothes on the guard in front of the fire to keep them warm and dry for the next day. Unfortunately, a live coal had dropped on to the hearth and it made contact with the clothes. By some miracle, they did not catch fire, but simply emitted clouds of smoke, there were no flames. We prevented any further smoke by stamping on the clothes. We then opened all doors and windows and, at last, sat down breathless and exhausted. What a narrow escape!

After making sure that everything was quite safe, we went to bed, but it was a long time before I fell into a very troubled sleep. I am sure that all the other members of the family had the same problem as my father did not go to work the next day; he was too upset. Besides, his working clothes were in ruins and never again were clothes put before the fire! Strangely enough, I was given no credit for the part I had played in this accident. I was deeply hurt! For if I had not awakened when I did, the house would have eventually gone up in flames!Light in the house was by a solitary oil lamp in the centre of the kitchen table. It was, indeed, a poor light, leaving dark corners in the room. The streets in the town were lit by gas supplied by the local Urban District Council who had a gas works in that part of the town called Britannia. I do not know why we also did not have gas. It was either because we could not afford it, or that the council had not yet finished the task of supplying the whole town. We eventually had gas installed, but I cannot remember when.

The Council employed a man called 'the Lighter Man' to light the lamps in the night and to put them out in the morning. Armed with a long pole with a tiny hook at the top, he would perform this task with an expertise born of long practice. With hardly an upward glance, he would insert the top of the pole into an aperture in the lantern, give a little twist to the hook and lo!, the light would come on immediately. He would then resume his walk with hardly a backward glance. Some of the bolder spirits of the boys would endeavour to climb the lamp post to put out the light by hand, but no one ever succeeded because the lamp post column was too smooth and they could not find a hand or foot hold.

In the night, because they were the only lit places in the darkness, boys would congregate around the lamps and generally indulge in some horseplay. If it became too boisterous, it would attract the attention of the local policeman. He would take off his belt and run after them, belabouring them with all his might until he had cleared the place. The boys would not dare to complain to their parents about this treatment because it was highly likely that they would receive another hiding.

We were mortally afraid of policemen and always tried to avoid them, even sometimes running away to escape their notice when completely innocent. It was easy to maintain law and order in those days.

Gas was eventually installed in our house and then electricity in the early 1930s. What a boon! Improved lighting! Noiseless! No more striking matches to light the gas mantle. No more hissing of the mantle as it was approaching the last days of its active life. Just switch on – just switch off. Easy!

Our meals seemed to be adequate in quantity but unvaried and possibly lacking in some of the necessary vitamins. Twice a week, we had for our main meal what we called "taters and meat". No extra vegetables; utter extravagance! This meal was taken about 4.30 in the afternoon after we had returned from school. My father would eat earlier, at about 3.30, after returning from work. Twice a week we also had a meal of Welsh broth, the meat being shin beef or best end of the neck which was, of course, mutton. This was accompanied by various vegetables and lasted two days. On the second day it was much tastier than the first. We had fish on Friday; generally hake, which seems to have disappeared from today's menus. No chips! Too much preparation and my mother simply could not afford the time.

On Sunday, the main meal was eaten at midday. This was the only meal of the week when the family ate together, our father being present. Consequently, the meal was eaten in utter silence. The meals during the rest of the week were generally noisy, riotous affairs with petty squabbles and children noisily clamouring for more. This Sunday meal was more elaborate and consisted of a roast joint with an extra vegetable added to the inevitable potato. There were never any 'afters' or pudding after any of these main meals – again, utter extravagance! On Saturdays we had sausages with some leftover to provide my elder brother and myself with one sausage each for supper.

On Sunday mornings, we had another treat – one boiled egg to be shared between my brother and myself. What riches! I always complained that my brother seemed to have the larger portion. My brother argued that it was a fair arrangement as he was older and bigger than I. I could see some justice in this argument but I always resented it.

One Saturday night, my father brought home for supper what he thought was a great treat – a piece of tripe. Only my brother and I were present, the younger children being sent to bed earlier. This piece of tripe either was a poor specimen or my mother did not know how to cook it, but the result was horrible. A piece of tough leather and my brother and I promptly rejected it. My father, disappointed to see this so called treat meeting such a reception, became very angry and, raising his voice, said, "You'll stay at the table until you finish it". My brother and I looked at each other mournfully and kept on chewing manfully, until with a thankful gulp, the last morsel disappeared. Tripe never appeared on the menu again.

The rest of the meals, generally consisted for the most part of bread and butter. There was sometimes jam and cheese, mostly Cheddar. We were never allowed the luxury of bread and butter and jam, or bread and butter and cheese. Oh! No! Where do you think the money is coming from to buy such luxuries? We had to be content with bread and butter, bread and jam, or bread and cheese.

Biscuits were unknown, cake a rarity. Sometimes in the summer my mother would bake some apple or rhubarb tart. It was rather curious that, although most of the miners' gardens were uncultivated, many contained rhubarb plants. These were very bitter in taste and the leaves were green and tough. However, we improved matters by putting a bucket with a large hole in the bottom, upside down on the plant, completely covering it, giving a shelter akin to a miniature hot house. The result was eminently satisfactory. The leaves turned pale green, the stems a delicate pink and the taste much sweeter. It made a very edible dish. We gave the name of "plate cake" to all tarts.

We were very fond of my mother's homemade bread which she made twice weekly. It was beautifully white with an appetising crust. It was baked in the local bake house or 'bacws' and it was my task to deliver and collect it. I did this very reluctantly on cold winter nights. The baker would open the oven door, sending a welcome breath of hot air through the bake house. Armed with a long pole at the end of which was a ladle which he would thrust into the depths of the intensely hot oven and with a dexterity born of long practice, would insert the ladle under each loaf which he would swiftly withdraw and place on a stone shelf to cool. This would take about ten minutes and then impatient to be gone, I would pay the baker. Tucking a tin under each arm giving a comforting warmth to my whole body, I would sally forth on my long journey home. Before leaving home to perform this very important errand, my mother would give me strict instructions not to pick at the crust on the way back. She know quite well that I would disobey, not being able to resist a tasty morsel and I know that she knew, but there seemed to be a tacit understanding that I should be allowed to do some picking, provided that it was not excessive, just as a reward for performing this very essential errand. But she was careful not to make it a spoken arrangement.

A thought has come into my mind as I write these lines. Where was my elder brother and what was he doing when I performed these errands? Perhaps being nearly five years older than I, he was engaged in more important and onerous tasks. On looking back, he always seems to me to present a very shadowy figure, hovering around the outermost limits of my life.

Puddings were not the usual accompaniments to our main meal, we simply did without. On the occasions in the summer when my mother made fruit tart, it was served as a special treat as our Sunday treat at tea time; bought or shop cake never figured in our menu. We could not afford such luxury.

Sometimes during the summer months, those of us who had the energy, went to pick whimberries on the mountain slopes. We took our father's tommy box to hold the fruit after it had been gathered. It was a heartbreaking task. The fruit was very small, just as tiny as blackcurrants and it grew on the surface of the grass. We had to lie prone on the ground to pick them and it took a long time even to cover the bottom of the tommy box, small though it was. Often we would shout at one another, "Have you covered the bottom yet?" I don't think that any one of us ever succeeded in filling the box to its brim. It was also imperative to wear our oldest clothes as the whimberries were apt to stain them with a deep purple colour, which was very difficult to eradicate. Whimberry picking was not, therefore, a favourite pastime, and once a summer was quite enough. After we had eaten them, the insides of our mouths remained quite purple for a considerable time, but the fruit made a delicious tart.

Fresh fruit was a rarity and not very varied. There were apples, the most common variety was called Morgan Sweets and were almost tasteless. Oranges did not appear until about Christmas time. They were Spanish, very small and very bitter. The favourite fruit was bananas which were used in sandwiches for my lunch when I went to the Grammar School. Tomatoes did not appear until late summer and the more exotic fruits like peaches, apricots, even strawberries, were never seen.

Sometimes my father would send us to buy a pennorth of damaged apples. These were long past their 'sell by' date. The fruiterer would cut out the damaged parts and put what was left on display. For one penny we could buy enough apples for the whole family.

Those of the inhabitants who took the trouble to cultivate their gardens generally had gooseberry and blackcurrant bushes growing, of which could also fill delicious tarts.

We bought our milk at the door. The milkman would arrive on foot with his can of milk on, which hung two cans, a half-pint, the other a whole pint. He would give a loud knock at the door to which one of us would go with a jug to purchase a happorth of milk. Milk was a penny a pint. This was enough to supply our needs for the whole day including a saucerful of milk for the family cat. This was the only regular meal we gave her during the day, but it was usually supplemented by scraps given by the children. Pet food was as yet unknown. In any case, we could not have afforded it even if it had existed. Even so, the cat was always lively and in good condition. She was left out at night except when it was cold or wet and during her nocturnal expeditions she must have been a mighty hunter, a good mouser.

There was no exchange of money with the milkman after the purchase. He would simply make a record in his account book, leaving the payment to be made at the end of the week. We were always short of money during the week until my father arrived home with his pay on Saturday afternoon. It was then my duty to take the payment to what was euphemistically called the dairy, which was a real misnomer because it was simply the flagstone scullery at the back of the milk round owner's house. The name of the milkman was Mike Griffiths, so, naturally, with the fondness of the valley people for nicknames, he was known as "Mike the Milk".

English people have often wondered about this Welsh fondness for nicknames and the explanation is quite simple. In the distant past, it was the custom to use the father's Christian name as the surname of his offspring, the new name being prefixed by the word 'ap' which means the 'offspring of'. Hence, if the son was given the name 'William' and his father's Christian name was' Thomas', the boy would be known as 'William ap Thomas'. Similarly, a daughter called 'Blodwen' would be called 'Blodwen ap Thomas'. However, as the number of Christian names was obviously very limited, it follows that the surnames would be few in number. Therefore, it was clear that some distinction had to be made, and this was done by adding another name – the nickname. This used some idiosyncrasy on the part of the owner or his job or where he lived. For example, if I came home one day and said to my mother, "I saw Mrs Jones in town this morning", she would immediately ask, "Which Mrs Jones?" (there being so many Mrs Jones'). I would then say, "Mrs Jones Yellow Hat" and she would immediately know which person I meant – this particular Mrs Jones always wore a yellow hat. In the course of time, the prefix 'ap' gradually fell out of use, although, at the present moment with the attempt to revive the Welsh language, some fervent Welsh men have begun to use it once more.

Some nicknames were very appropriate, some ridiculous and others plain silly. Some were superfluous, for example, in the case of the aforesaid Mike Griffiths, the addition of the nickname 'the Milk' was not needed as the mention of only the name was enough to indicate who it was.

Some nicknames were very appropriate. For example, 'Annie Walk nice' (for a lady with a dainty, mincing walk); 'Martha Jane Fussy' – self explanatory, real name; 'Mrs Thomas Wedi Danto' – a lady who complained continually of the many misfortunes which beset her and who said that she was daunted thereby; 'Sally Swc' – lady who kept on suckling her babies long after the usual time; 'Tommy Teacher' – a native of the place who became a teacher and who taught me in Standard 4 and 5, real name Thomas Williams; 'The Black Bishop' – brother of the aforesaid Thomas Williams called 'Black' because he had very black hair and a dark complexion. 'Mr Jenkins Pretty Whiskers' – another teacher who sported a luxuriant black moustache; 'Dafydd Siwgr' – rumoured that he had told his wife that her kisses were as sweet as sugar. He, incidentally was one of the miners entombed in the Tynewydd pit disaster mentioned earlier, real name David Jenkins; 'John The Cobbler' – one of the many brothers of Gwyn Thomas the writer and a contemporary of mine in the primary school; 'Shoni One Eye' – self explanatory, real name John Richards; 'Ben the Gardener' – mentioned earlier; 'Morgan City Tailors' – owner of a tailor's shop in the main street where we had our best suits measured and fitted and where my younger sister, Nana, worked as a seamstress for a short while before she was taken ill; 'Will Mam' – a man living in Tylorstown who married his mother-in-law some time after his wife's death; 'Dai Two Suits' – it was customary for a man to have only one suit for evening wear, but this man had two which he wore on alternative evenings. He was much envied; 'Tom Short Walk' – when going out, "I am only going for a short walk" he would say, but he was invariably out for hours, having walked miles; 'Johnny BSc' - one of the few men in those days who took a degree at the university and who later became a contemporary of mine at the Porth County School as a chemistry master; 'Hannah Bananas' – a lady from Pontygwaith who was for some time a great friend of Hannah's brother, Willie, but nothing came of it. Why 'Bananas' was never explained to me, real name Hannah Jenkins.

Some of the Valley humorists, eager to show their sense of humour would invent nicknames of their own such as; 'Dai Upper Crust'. Dai the baker was initially known as Dai Crust because he had always made lovely crusty bread. One day, the Queen visited the area and during one of her walkabouts, she had a long chat with Dai. Henceforward, he was known as Dai Upper Crust. 'Dai Bungalow' – a man was thus nicknamed because he was slow-witted with nothing upstairs; 'Dai Central (H)eating' – man who had only two teeth in his mouth right in the centre, one pointing north and the other south. These names are just examples of the Valley people poking fun at themselves.

Two names, real names this time, are worthy of note. When I was teaching in the Porth County School, there was a boy in one class whose name was Karl Lenin Dolling. His father, George Dolling, a check weigher at the local colliery, was Communist and a Marxist. He therefore called his son Karl after Karl Marx and Lenin, of course, after Lenin. Poor boy! Another pupil at the school was 'Posthumous Evans' so called because he was born after his father had died.

It has just occurred to me that I have mentioned the word 'check weigher' in describing the job of George Dolling. There were 2 check weighers assigned to every pit. When the miner at the coal face had filled his tram with coal, he chalked his number on the side which then, accompanied by other miners' full trams was pulled by a pony in charge of a man called the haulier, to the pit bottom. It was then hoisted in the cage to the pithead where it was awaited by the 2 check weighers. One represented the owners and one the miners, and they weighed the trams then recorded the weight on the miner's wage bill. George Dolling, of course, was the miner's representative. One can hardly imagine the owners appointing a Communist as their representative.

I digress. To come back to names. If you were blessed with two Christian names, both were used when you were addressed, with one of them usually abbreviated. My brother's names were William John, named after his father and grandfather, abbreviated when he was addressed to Willie John. His uncle's name, Thomas John was abbreviated to Tommy John. A boy next door to us, Thomas William was called Tommy Willie. Both names in this case were abbreviated which was rather unusual.

Some parents repeated their surname in the son's Christian name. For example, William Williams, Thomas Thomas, Evan Evans, but Richard Richards reached the height of absurdity when it was abbreviated, to 'Double Dick'.

If your father bellowed your two Christian names in full, Thomas John, for example, you knew that you were in trouble. When so called, you dropped everything and scuttled off in great haste to present yourself to the august presence of his majesty, usually to account for some misdemeanour on your part and to receive a severe reprimand with a threat of dire punishment if repeated.

Central heating was an amenity of the future. We went to bed by candlelight to unheated bedrooms, which became icy cold in the winter. If you went to bed with cold feet, they remained cold all night. If you were unlucky to be born on a winter's night, a frosty reception indeed!

There was no central heating, there was no hot water system and all water had to be boiled on the coal fire, either in a kettle, bucket or boiler. Hot water for shaving, hot water for tea, hot water for washing dishes after a meal, kettle on the fire; hot water for bathing or washing clothes, bucket or boiler on the fire. Baking or cooking was done in the oven adjoining the fire.

On bath night, which was usually Friday, a tin bath was placed on the mat in front of the fire with the bottom filled with cold water to which was added hot water which had been heated in a bucket on the fire. In we tumbled, one by one, all five of us being bathed in the same water. The state of the water for the fifth bather was matter for conjecture, but it did not matter a great deal for the fifth was the eldest and therefore the cleanest. Then we were dispatched in turn to bed after a meagre supper of bread and butter and a glass of water, leaving our mother tired and exhausted and no doubt heaving a sigh of relief as she saw the last one disappearing up the stairs. My father never seems to have been present at this weekly ritual. Perhaps he deemed it expedient to be absent in case he would be asked to help. But he need not have worried, for in that male dominant world it was considered unmanly for any male to do household tasks, even washing dishes after a meal. Looking back over the years, it seems incredible to me that my mother was able to lift those heavy buckets without mishap. Life was very hard for a woman in those days.

Washing day on Monday was another arduous day for the housewife. A tin bath, or wooden tub was placed on a bench and then filled with hot water into which some soap powder was poured. Then was produced a washing board with a metal corrugated sheet, against which she would rub the clothes until clean. Then the clothes were taken to be hung on the clothesline which was extended between two posts at either end of the garden and which was held up in the middle by a prop with a V-shape cleft at the top.

When the clothes were considered dry enough, they were taken into the house for ironing in the kitchen. If thought to be too dry, they were sprinkled with drops of cold water. The irons were very heavy, being indeed made of iron. They were heated either on top of or in the oven adjoining the coal fire. Temperature was gauged by the housewife spitting on the iron. If the spittle sizzled, the heat was considered satisfactory. Two irons were used, one being heated while the other was used. Then the clothes were placed to be aired on a temporary line extended between two corners of the kitchen; there was no airing cupboard. However, the process of airing on the line did not take long because the kitchen always had a good fire, even on the hottest day, otherwise we should have been without hot water.

It was the custom in those days for baby boys and baby girls to be dressed exactly alike. I have, at present, a photograph of myself thus attired, sitting on a chair with my elder brother, then aged about five years, standing at my side. I wore a dress or frock and my hair was rather long. When the boy reached the age of one year or thereabouts and was able to walk, he was 'britched' as the Valley people termed it. That is, the dress was discarded in favour of a pair of short trousers with the addition of a pair of socks, which left the knees exposed to the weather. The upper part of the body was clothed in a jersey, dark in colour.

At about 11 years of age, the jersey was replaced by a jacket topped by an India rubber collar, which we had to wash every morning before we went to school. On special occasions, the boy wore a linen collar, but the occasion had to be special because, after a day's wear, this type of collar had to be sent to the laundry. That process cost money, so precious in those days. The short trousers in due course were replaced by a knickerbocker type of trousers buttoned below the knees, protecting them from the weather. Instead of socks, they boy wore stockings, always dark in colour. I have a photograph of myself so attired, when I was in Form I in the Grammar School, together with my friend, Elvet Jones.

At about 15 years of age, we graduated to what we called long trousers and then we thought that we had really grown up. We

Ivor at five years of age with elder brother

wore a jacket and also a collar and tie. The shirt and collar were not in one piece as they are today, but were quite separate and both usually white. There was no top button on the shirt, it being replaced by a stud. There was a buttonhole at the back of the top of the shirt with a corresponding buttonhole at the back of the collar. In each buttonhole was inserted a small bone stud which prevented the collar rising in the back above the shirt, a very complex arrangement which took some time in adjusting and was a complete nuisance in the morning when we were in a hurry. Looking back, I often wonder why we did not adopt the simpler arrangement of today.

Footwear for boys was heavy and substantial, boots – not shoes – amply provided with hobnails supplemented by iron tips at heels and toes. The leather was exceedingly stiff when new, and until broken in by constant use, chaffed against the skin causing a red rough ring just above the ankle, very painful, especially in cold weather. We tried to soften stiffness by applying what was called 'shoe oil' with a brush. This process was never very successful and, at times, could prove a nuisance because unless applied very sparingly the oil would refuse to dry by the morning. Boys cleaned their own boots by applying 'blacking' using two brushes, one for application and the other for polishing. This job was performed in the lobby and had to be done thoroughly, for unless they had a gleaming shine, bright enough to satisfy the searching scrutiny of our mother, it had to be done over again.

We found that if we scraped the sole and heel forcibly and swiftly along the pavement, the boot would emit a shower of bright sparks. Indeed, some boys became so adept at this trick creating such a shower of sparks that it looked as if the boot would at any moment, burst into flames. Naturally our parents frowned on this practice, which caused unnecessary wear. So, we played this game out of sight and sound of home. Competition to produce the most sparks was very keen.

When boots needed repair, they were taken to the local shoemaker, Jim Samuel. He had established his workshop in the front room of his house and worked at the window for light. He was very swift and adept at his work and we would often stop to gaze wonderingly at his performance. He was in the habit of keeping the small nails, called 'sprigs', in his mouth in order to speed up their transference to the boot to be hammered in. We were very concerned that one-day he would have the misfortune to swallow them. Jim had a sense of humour and sometimes he would pretend that this had actually happened and went into paroxysms of choking, while we outside would gaze, open-mouthed, uncertain whether he was teasing or not. But Jim would recover rapidly, and the performance ended. He would wave us away, and much relieved, we would scamper off on our travels.

Looking back, it should have been obvious that Jim Samuel performed his pantomimic charade only when his mouth was empty of nails. In our innocent minds, although we had suspicions, we were never quite sure, which Jim knew only too well. We were always relieved when Jim made his miraculous recovery and the charade never seemed to pall on us!

On Sundays and special occasions we would wear lighter footwear, and when I started to attend the Grammar School, I permanently discarded the heavy boots.

The family next door to us at No. 4, Thomas by name, boasted a family even larger than ours, eight children all told. The father, Ned Thomas, was a short, stocky man, very dark, beetle-browed, savage and fierce in countenance. He was hardly ever seen and when he deigned to appear, his words were few. He maintained a rigid discipline and the frequent yells heard coming from the house would indicate that he was administering punishment, usually with his belt. The children seemed to thrive on this treatment, all strong and healthy, rarely ill.

The second eldest was a boy of about my age, Arthur, and our relationship varied from strong, apparently eternal friendship to one of bitter enmity. When enemies, we would stand on our respective doorsteps and make faces at each other, in Valley dialect, making 'jibs'. He was good at it and would twist his features into such grotesque grimaces that I often wondered if he would get them back into their original shape. I would try to compete with him, but was left far behind. It was no contest! He would best Les Dawson himself at this game! I would console myself that he had a start on me because I was better looking and in retrospect, I think that there was some justification for this belief for he was no beauty, just his father in miniature.

Visiting the Doctor's

As is usual with families, we had our share of cuts and bruises, falls and accidents, although it seemed I escaped very lightly, perhaps because I was not very venturesome. Early in my life, too early for me to remember, my parents told me that I had fallen against the kitchen fender and sustained a deep cut on the chin, just below the lower lip. When it eventually healed, it left a scar, which remained with me until it disappeared after my lip operation for carcinoma in 1984. It was a blue scar, like a miner's scar, and I often wondered whether some coal dust from the air had entered during the healing process.

Later in life, I was pushing a small cart before me on the pavement outside our house when I stumbled and, unable to save myself, I fell forward with my chin hitting the pavement with a heavy thud. I got up yelling with pain and my yelling grew even louder when, thoroughly frightened, I found my mouth full of blood. I rushed frantically home, where on examining my mouth, my mother was horrified to find, not only a flood of blood, but also a hole in the middle of my tongue where my teeth had made a deep penetration. Panic stricken and fearing that I would lose my powers of speech, she speedily hustled me off to the doctor's surgery. The doctor, having made a thorough examination was unperturbed. "Not to worry," he said, "the tongue is the quickest part of the body to heal. In a week's time the hole will have completely disappeared." And so it proved. Great rejoicing! My parents would not have a dumb child on their hands after all.

The surgery, was not far away from our home. The practice consisted of three doctors, and the fees were paid by a weekly deduction from my father's wages made by the colliery offices. Non mining families paid their fees by annual subscription. The senior doctor, Dr Jackson, was tall, saturnine, immaculately groomed. We saw very little of him. Rumour had it, no doubt unfairly, that he spent most of his time attending to the fee paying families who were better off than the mining families.

The second doctor, Dr Lionel Lewis, was a bluff, outspoken man, very well liked by his patients. The name Lionel was foreign to Valley ears, so he was known as Dr Lilie. When he visited miners' homes, he spoke the miners' rough language, including some swear words. An amusing story which was told, about his visit to Mrs Edwards. Mrs Edwards was an old lady who was almost monoglot Welsh. She had asked the doctor to call to see her husband. He had a very bad throat and when asked by the doctor what was the matter with her husband, she either did not know or had forgotten the English word for 'throat', but she knew the word for 'neck'. She replied, very hesitatingly, "He's got a neck, doctor". Dr Lilie, very amused, replied, "Has he indeed?! I'm very glad of that. He would look bloody funny without one."

The third doctor, Doctor Edwards, was a short man with a white moustache and a very red face. He looked much older than the other two because of his white moustache. To him seemed to fall the most humdrum and menial tasks, including tooth extraction, at which he was expert. Tooth decay was very prevalent in those days, due not only to the excessive consumption of sweet foodstuffs in our diet, but also to the lack of necessary vitamins in our monotonous

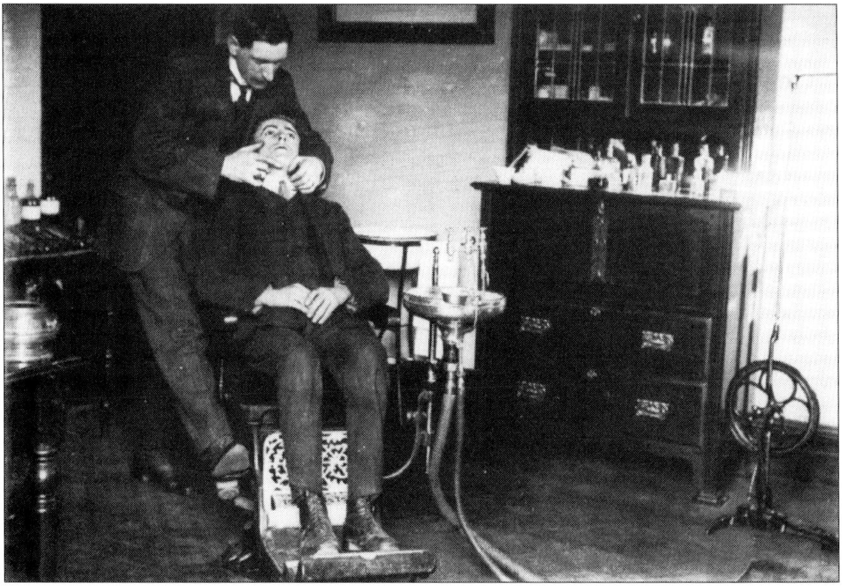

Dentist's Surgery - 1910

(Photograph published by Glamorgan Archive Service)

meals. There was one dentist in town, but very few could afford the fee. Dentistry was in its infancy in those days, there was no certainty that the process would be pain free as recourse was made to an extraction 'in the raw', that is without any anaesthetic.

The lad affected would be brought to the surgery; always by his father, the mother being unequal to this task. They would be shown into a small anteroom specially set apart for this kind of examination. Dr Edwards would be waiting and would say, "Open your mouth". The boy, very wary and uncertain as to what was going to happen, would hesitatingly half open his mouth at which the doctor would say, "Come on! Open wider, I'm only going to examine the tooth". The boy would obediently open wide and before he knew what was happening, he was uttering the most bloodcurdling cries. The doctor's forceps, craftily concealed up his sleeve, was already at work pulling at the offending molar. Patients in the waiting room would wince in sympathy on hearing these heartbreaking cries. Suddenly, the cries would cease followed by ominous silence. The door would open and out would emerge the father, looking very relieved, followed closely by the boy, more relieved, but also aggrieved because he had been so blatantly deceived. Last of all would come Dr Edwards, triumphantly waving the bloodstained forceps with the offending molar in its clutches. "There!" the doctor would exclaim, "It wasn't so bad after all, was it?" If looks could kill, he would have died where he stood, but he was a real expert at his job.

The surgery consisted of a waiting room, a consulting room, the anteroom just mentioned and another small room called the dispensary where all medicines were kept and which was the domain of Dr Williams, the dispenser. He was called Dr Williams, but that was only a courtesy title as he was not qualified. He was a small, slight man, brusque in manner and never saying a word. Outdoors he always wore a dirty raincoat and bowler hat. He was a bachelor and lived either alone or in lodgings.

Procedure was as follows. You waited in the waiting room until your name was called. You then entered the consulting room, explained your symptoms to the doctor, had yourself diagnosed or perhaps examined if deemed necessary and then handed a paper with the name of the medicine prescribed which you handed to Dr Williams. There was no prescription for the chemist because there was no N.H.S. It occurs to me that there were hardly ever any tablets or capsules prescribed, but only medicines and there appeared to be very few of these because I can only remember two – a red medicine for coughs and colds and a pinkish-white for stomach ailments.

Dr Williams was a man of mystery while he lived, and his end was equally mysterious. One day, he disappeared, vanished into thin air like a puff of smoke, not a sign of him anywhere. One day he was there as usual; next day he had disappeared without a word of explanation. He was a lonely man and had no known relations to be informed and consulted. As time went on, people gave up wondering, Dr Williams was gradually forgotten and a new dispenser appointed.

There was a sequel and an explanation of the mystery surrounding Dr Williams' disappearance many years later. A leak was discovered in the surgery roof, which let in water when it rained. Local builders were consulted. The firm consisted of a man called Hopkins and his three sons, two of whom accordingly arrived. The youngest, Mansel, was sent up to investigate. On emerging into the attic from the top of the ladder, in the half-light of his torch he saw Dr Williams attired in his usual bowler hat and dirty raincoat sitting on a chair, apparently asleep. Mansel gingerly put out a tentative hand to awake him, but at the slightest touch of his hand, Dr Williams suddenly collapsed, on the attic floor, a heap of bones, topped by bowler hat and raincoat.

Terrified and horror stricken, Mansel rushed down the ladder to the lower room, fell into a chair and wiped his sweat covered brow. He could do nothing more than babble, almost incoherently, with his finger pointing upwards. "Up there! Up there!" His brother rushed up the ladder to discover to his horror what Mansel had already seen. A heap of bones mingled with a raincoat and bowler hat. The mystery was solved! Dr Williams had committed suicide in the attic. His life had been quiet and lonely, his death equally so.

Poor Mansel was rushed home, too upset to continue and it was a few days before he recovered. No doubt, he would always remember that macabre incident, event to his dying day.

The Library - Books and Billiards

The deduction from my father's pay to settle the doctors' fees was not the only one. He also contributed a few pence a week to a fund which had been set up to repay a loan made by the bank to build a library and institute for the miners. The institute was a substantial, stone built, two storey building in the centre of the village. It had a rather imposing entrance, which led to an equally imposing entrance hall on each side of which were two large rooms; two reading rooms, a games room and a library. From the entrance hall, a wide staircase led to the upper floor which contained a huge room extending along the whole length of the building, a billiards room with two billiard tables. This was used for Union meetings and mass meetings of the miners whenever a crisis occurred.

One of the reading rooms downstairs was devoted to newspapers, both national and local. These were placed on newspaper stands where one could read them either standing or seated on high stools. The other reading room provided an abundance of periodicals and magazines.

In the games room, there was provision for card playing, dominoes, draughts and chess. Table tennis was unknown in those days. This room, intended for the younger element, though sparsely attended in the summer, provided a convenient warm meeting place for the young bloods of the village to congregate in the winter, not only for games, but also for juvenile gossip, teasing and leg pulling, plus a little horseplay. If this became too obstreperous, it ended in ejection by the librarian. The leg pulling was directed against people's deficiencies and failings and could sometimes be very cruel as was common in juvenile circles. There was one boy, John Jones, about twelve or thirteen years of age, of ponderous build, slow in movement and equally slow witted, an easy butt for practical jokes. He would be sent on impossible errands, such as "John, go down to the dairy and ask for a pennorth of pigeon's milk and tell her that your mother will pay at the end of the week", or, "John, go to the newsagents and ask for a copy of the Grave-digger's Gazette". The shopkeepers concerned would know very well what was happening and would give John a polite, non committal answer. Poor John! Because of his ponderous build, slow movements and slow wits, he was cruelly nicknamed 'John Elephant Jones'.

The billiard room was very well patronised, especially during winter evenings. The usual game was billiards. Snooker, which has become very popular these days because of extensive television coverage, was played only occasionally by way of a change. This preference was very strange because, in my opinion, snooker is a far more interesting game. As with most games, young people had their heroes in billiards too, Tom Newman, Melbourne Inman and George Gray. Tom Newman was a very skilful player, a real artist in his work and it was a pleasure to see him play. Billiards is a game, which demands great concentration and perfect quiet. Newman, however, was of a very temperamental nature and could easily be put off his game by snide remarks from his opponent of which the latter always took full advantage. Melbourne Inman, on the other hand, although not so skilful, was a totally different character and was never upset. George Gray was very efficient, thorough and a scoring machine, but rather monotonous in his play. He was an Australian domiciled in England.

There were many like institutes in villages up and down the Valley, all provided with billiard rooms, so it was natural for them to compete with one another. A league was formed in which each institute chose a team. In the Cymmer Institute the best player was Will Griffiths, skilful, and a pleasure to watch when in form. But, like Tom Newman, he was very temperamental. There was also Dewi Davies, after the style of Melbourne Inman, who won many of his matches by upsetting his opponent with disparaging remarks.

The nearest institute, Ynyshir, were very keen rivals and doughty opponents. The matches against them were always of a needle character. On one occasion, it was a very equal contest; it was obvious that the issue would not be decided until the last game in which the opponents were Dewi Davies and Morgan (Mog) Benjamin, men of like character, good talkers and formidable foes. As the game went on, it became apparent that Ynyshir were going to win. Dewi, for once, was being out talked and as Mog Benjamin, cue in hand, was poised over the table to make the winning shot, the lights suddenly went out! Somebody downstairs, acting on a signal from someone standing on the landing outside the billiard room upstairs had turned off the main! Result – shouts, yells, curses, cues and billiard balls thrown about the place.

Discretion being the best part of valour, I hurriedly quit the scene. What happened afterwards I know not. If the match was going to be replayed, I intended not to be present.

The institute library was a revelation and a godsend to me. Whoever performed the task of furnishing it did a magnificent job. It contained books of every description, fiction, biographies, books on history and geography, science and religion. The books were bound in hard leather covers, able to withstand years of usage and were kept in huge glass cupboards with sliding doors.

Hitherto, my reading had been confined to the comic papers, all very popular. One was called *Comic Cuts* with the chief character on the front page called 'Tom, the Ticket of Leave Man'. 'The Ticket of Leave' was given to prisoners released on probation. Another paper was called *Chips* with the chief characters 'Weary Willie' and 'Tired Tim'. A third paper was called *Merry and Bright* which, for some reason, I persisted in calling "Mary Ann Bright" much to the amusement of my elders, so much so that my Uncle Bob, an inveterate leg-puller, sent me a postcard to 'Miss Mary Ann Bright'.

My father took a daily newspaper called *The Daily News*, which was later amalgamated with *The Daily Chronicle* to be called *The News Chronicle*, all liberal in outlook. The Labour paper, *The Daily Herald* did not appear until much later. To the astonishment of my elders, I was able to read the newspapers at a very early age. My mother was also an eager reader and took a weekly woman's magazine called *Woman's Weekly*, price one penny. As far as I can remember, my father never read a book in his life, but, strangely enough, occasionally he bought a weekly magazine called *Boxing*. My grandparents bought no daily newspaper, but took a weekly one called *The Police News* whose front page always featured lurid scenes such as men lying on the floor in pools of blood with their throats cuts.

The library changed all my reading habits and my mother's also. I used to bring home books to her written by an author called Mrs Henry Woods, the Catherine Cookson of her time. One of her many books was the popular *East Lynne* which contained the famous concluding, tear-jerking lines, "Dead! Dead! and never called me mother!" which brought many an enjoyable tear to women's eyes.

I became an avid reader of the library books. At the age of ten or eleven, adventure stories were the favourites and R.M. Ballantyne and G.H. Henty the favourite authors. In these books figured handsome heroes, as brave as lions, unafraid of all danger, always engaged in stern struggles against the forces of evil. In my imagination, I followed these heroes all over the world, to the prairies of the Middle West of America, to the tropical forests of Brazil, to the blue lagoons of the Mediterranean, the snow capped peaks of the Himalayas and the barren steppes of Siberia. From all these struggles we emerged victorious, leaving the enemy ignominiously defeated.

Indeed, so engrossed was I in some of these books that I actually finished them in one day to the astonishment and disbelief of the librarian. At first, he remained unpersuaded that I had returned them so soon because I did not like them. In the end, however, I managed to convince him otherwise. At last, he came to the belief that he had an exceptional reader on his hands and took very kindly to me, often patting my head encouragingly as I left the building, eagerly clutching the precious book in my hands in joyful anticipation of the pleasures to come in following another hero all over the world.

The librarian's name was Joseph (Joe) Thomas, a disabled miner whose days in the mine were ended by an horrific accident. He lived in a house conveniently placed adjoining the library which had been built by the miners for him and all future librarians.

There was also an assistant librarian named William (Bill) Gwyn who was also a disabled miner. He acted more as a caretaker than a librarian. The affairs of the whole institute were managed by a committee elected annually by the miners.

Street Games and Corner Shops

Modern day youth complain that they have recourse to mischief because they have nothing to occupy their time, and that not enough provision is made for their entertainment. We in our age had no such complaint because we provided our own entertainment and thoroughly enjoyed it. In any case we could not have afforded computer games or videos nor did we have any desire to spend our time cooped up in our bedrooms when we could be out of doors enjoying the fresh air.

The games we played were many and various. The younger boys played 'Hook and Wheel' in which they ran for miles without knowing it, so engrossed were they in their game. They also played 'Whip and Top', which entailed some degree of practical skill attained only by constant practice. The bigger boys played 'Weak Horses, Strong Donkeys', a real rough and tumble game. There were games like 'Whistle or Holler' and 'Dicky, Show Light', which were played during the dark winter evenings. There was also 'Marbles', of which there were many variations. A favourite game was 'Catty and Dog', the dog being a short stick about arm's length with which we hit the catty, a much shorter stick with pointed ends. Football occupied a low priority because we had never seen a real football in our lives and if we had, we could not afford one. It was only rarely that we could afford a small rubber ball. We also played a type of cricket called 'French Cricket' which could be played if one of us had been bought a bat as a Christmas present, a very rare occurrence indeed.

Our favourite game was 'Cowboys and Indians'. The fights we fought were fierce with the inevitable result that the cowboys were always victorious and stranger still, with no casualties. The Indians, on the other hand, were completely wiped out, leaving no survivors. The boys who played Indians were superb actors, especially a boy called Sam Adams. He always died a slow, agonising death, so slow that we, the cowboys, got tired of waiting for his last moments and moved on leaving him to die alone. This treatment of his superb acting so incensed Sam that he would suddenly come to life again, upraiding us for a lack of well deserved sympathy. It was therefore decided that Sam should, from now on, take a permanent part of a cowboy, and as cowboys never sustained any casualties, we should never have to undergo the ordeal of waiting to see him die. The boys generally took alternate parts – cowboy one day would become an Indian the next and vice-versa. Sam reluctantly agreed to this arrangement and we thought we had satisfactorily settled the problem, but we had forgotten that Sam was a very wily character.

In the next fight, the unexpected and unprecedented happened. A cowboy had been severely wounded and was rolling about in agony, giving a superb performance! Who was it? Of course, we ought to have known, it was Sam! Who else? The fight was immediately stopped and Sam given his marching orders, never again to be a cowboy or Indian. So Sam left our scene in high dudgeon. Thus was a superb actor lost to the world. No doubt, Laurence Olivier would have been delighted to hear the news. A formidable rival out of the way.

The girls, naturally, played more gentle games, from which boys were expressly forbidden. The favourites were hopscotch, skipping, Puss in the Corner, The Bells of St. Clements, Three Jolly Welshmen.

The younger collier boys played card games for pennies on the lower slopes of the mountainside. Card games for money were strictly illegal unless played on premises licensed for that purpose. A strict watch for delinquents was kept by the local policeman. There were no speedy cars with flashing lights and klaxons in those days, but simply a village Bobby who had a thorough knowledge of the district. He knew the troublemakers and if there was trouble, knew where to look for its source. The Bobby in our time was P.C. Taylor, a handsome well set up man with two equally handsome young sons, exact replicas of their father. They were strictly confined to the house premises and not allowed to mix with the miners' children.

The collier boys played their illicit card games behind a wall on the mountainside so as not to be seen from the road. As an extra precaution they posted a lookout, taking it in turns to do so. One day they were completely hoodwinked by a boy called Hughie Hughes, an elusive customer, as slippery as an eel, about two years older than our boys. He paid us only sporadic visits during which he looked in scorn on our childish games and did not hesitate to tell us. He was too old for his years by far.

One day he arrived among us proudly showing a policeman's helmet. Police helmets in our time were formidable objects with a spike on the crown similar to the German Army helmets during the First World War. We did not know where he got it from and did not want to know in case we were questioned later. He took us to the mountain side where the card games were being played, donned the helmet and crouched behind a low wall, now and again showing his head complete with helmet and raised the alarm, at which the players ran off in all directions. This was the signal for Hughie to appear in full view complete with helmet, shouting at the top of his voice and making contemptuous gestures at the fugitives. On looking back and seeing who it was, they stopped in their tracks and turned round to pursue the young rascal who had given them such a fright, but, in vain as Hughie was his usual elusive self. They hunted him for days, but he always eluded them. At last, they gave in, and seeing the funny side of the affair, laughed at their own discomfiture. Hughie was forgiven and was even at times enlisted as their scout during their card games. One mystery still remained – where did Hughie get the helmet? We preferred not to know. In the words of Thomas Gray, in his 'Ode to Eton College': 'Where ignorance is bliss, 'tis folly to be wise!'

The position of our street provided a suitable terrain for our games. There was a through road at each end of the street. The road at the top end of the street, called John Street because of its near vicinity to the church of St John, had not yet been taken over by the local Council and, consequently, it had not yet been made up. That being so, though being rather muddy in winter, it offered a firm surface in the summer and an ideal place for the children's games of which they took full advantage.

The third road ended in a cul de sac just below our house at No. 3, which provided a safe corner for the children. A further amenity was afforded when the corner house was converted into a shop by a local businessman called Morgan Hicks, an enterprising man, quick of speech and decisive in manner. He had already established a few shops of like nature in other parts of the town. They were a kind of general store selling mostly food. It was quite an imposing edifice with an enormous plate glass window extending practically the whole length of the house with a large entrance door at the end. The window was brilliantly lit in the hours of darkness and what was formerly a dark corner became as bright as day. There the children played to their hearts' content until the shop closed at 8 o'clock when the corner became dark again. What is more, they played in perfect safety of which their parents were well aware, relaxing contentedly at home knowing that their children were in no danger. There were no traffic accidents. Motor cars were things of the future and what little traffic there was during the hours of darkness was entirely horse-drawn whose approach was easily discerned and easily avoided. There were no muggings, rapes, kidnappings or gangs of louts looking for trouble. All was peaceful! What was more, the village Bobby never seemed to be far away and this fact was always very reassuring.

We lived in a law-abiding community. Crime was almost unknown. No one locked the house door during the day when they were absent for a while and at night only did so as force of habit more than fear of a break in. It was a closely-knit community and everybody knew everybody else. The few shady characters were well known to the local policeman. If a crime was committed, the culprit was sure to have been seen going to or coming from the scene of the crime. Strangers were looked on askance and with great curiosity, the inhabitants wondering who they were, what they were and why they were there. However, in such a community, news travels fast and in a short while, the whole purpose of the visit was known to all. There were no mysteries in our community.

The front door of our house was never shut, even in the depth of winter, as my mother was tired of opening and shutting it for the youngsters' continual comings and goings. The house was never cold, coal being so cheap, and we always had a huge fire in the grate, even in the middle of the summer, necessary for washing and cooking.

It is worthy of note that Mr Morgan Hicks had no need to apply for planning permission to convert the house into a shop, for the simple reason that there were no Planning Regulations. If one wished to convert, demolish or build, one simply went and did it; that was the end of the matter which sometimes makes one think that we are over-regulated at the present time. Uniformity means monotony and one has only to look at those monstrous tower blocks now happily being demolished to see that this is largely true. It is a pleasing contrast when one walks into a country village to see houses and cottages of different sizes, styles and colours.

Morgan Hicks' shop still exists, but shut and empty, having failed to compete with the supermarkets.

It is interesting to note, too, how the cost of living has risen due to the ravages of inflation. Compare these prices:

	1914	1996
1lb of beef	4p	£2.56
Large loaf	4p	70p
Quarter pound of tea	2p	45p
1lb of sugar	1p	35p
1 pint of milk	1p	36p
1/2 dozen eggs	3p	74p
Total cost of shopping	12p	£5.34

On summer evenings when the weather was pleasantly warm, the parents would venture forth into the open to view the children at play and at the same time obtain some much needed fresh air. The mother would be seated on a mat on the doorstep with the father sitting on his haunches beside – a favourite posture of the miners when at rest. It was a pleasant family scene with the children playing happily together and the parents viewing them with pride. Passers by would stop for a pleasant chat when all the latest news would be exchanged. The whole scene provided a feeling of comfort and security in a community to which one could turn for help in times of trouble.

Every summer, the street would be invaded by a flock of swallows or house martins that had nested in the eaves of the houses. They entertained us with their aerial acrobatics, soaring high in the air and sweeping down in a vertiginous descent only to soar back again, uttering shrill cries as if aware of an appreciative audience. Unfortunately, at the end of the summer, being migratory birds, they would leave us with dramatic suddenness. One day they were with us, entertaining as usual, the next they had gone, leaving us for more pleasant lands and sunnier shores. Our summers always seemed all too short, as Shakespeare observed in one of his poems, 'Summer's lease hath all too short a date'.

Sometimes of a summer evening, a group of mothers would gather their broods together and make their way up the lower slopes of the mountain, but a short walk away. The view was extensive. Behind were the steep slopes of the mountain whose summit rose to about 1100 feet above sea level, while immediately below could be seen the town, the railway to Cardiff, the river and the main road leading to Pontypridd. Directly opposite, rose the slopes of the other side of the valley, with rows of tiny miners' cottages clinging precipitously to the mountain side until they gave way to the bare slopes which soared on high above them. Here, while their mothers chatted together in warm friendship, the children played in complete happiness. Their favourite game was 'Roly Poly' which consisted of rolling down the mountain side until they reached the bottom with their heads whirling round and round in giddiness. As dusk started to fall, they made their way home, tired but happy.

Sometimes, during the school holidays, the older boys would light a small fire behind a low wall on the mountain side, out of sight of interfering adults, with dry twigs and some matches and pieces of old newspaper filched from the house unknown to their parents. On the fire they roasted potatoes, taken from the house. When finally roasted, the potatoes, though grubby in appearance, were delicious. No doubt, if the same potatoes were presented to them at the dinner table at home, they would have turned up their noses in distaste.

I was always curious about the mountain above us. It was never absent from sight. There it stood, a mighty giant, brooding in silent sadness over the folly of mortal beings that had desecrated the beauty of the valley beneath by greed. As I got older and stronger, I started to explore the mountain, always alone. It was strange that I never met anyone during the course of my wanderings.

The valley floor was about 200-300 feet above sea level, but the mountain (called Mynydd y Cymmer – Cymmer Mountain) rose to a height of 1100 feet with the result that the ascent was very steep. I always climbed the slope in direct ascent, scorning the many winding paths, which turned and twisted their way to the top. On the way up, my only company was the sheep grazing and ruminating in complete peace. I used to arrive at the top completely breathless after my steep climb, but this was soon forgotten as I gazed in wonder at the scene before my eyes. The summit did not end in a peak, but levelled itself out into an extensive plateau, which made walking very easy. In the middle of this was a large pool called the 'Lake', but it was not big enough to be so called. On a fine day, the pool waters shone like a large sheet of iridescent glass, and in the summer this was home to a small number of wading, aquatic birds whose cries accentuated the stillness of the air.

The mountain was part of the last of the ranges, which dominated the narrow mining valleys. On a clear day, on the southern side, could be seen the fertile fields and verdant plains of the Vale of Glamorgan, dotted with old world villages and the market towns of Bridgend and Cowbridge, with substantial farmhouses, surrounded by rich green fields on which herds of healthy cattle fed. The whole scene presented such a contrast to the grim mining valleys on the opposite side. Looking further afield, one could see the whole stretch of coastline from Swansea to Cardiff on which stood the seaside resorts of Porthcawl, Barry and Penarth. The coast was washed by the waters of the Bristol Channel with ships slowly sailing like toy boats. Just outside Cardiff were the twin islets of Steep Holm and Flat Holm, like two sentinels guarding the approaches to the port.

On the opposite side of the Bristol Channel was the coastline of Somerset and Devon with the seaside resorts of Minehead and Lynmouth, gradually giving way to the hills and mountains of Exmoor and Dartmoor.

Sadly, this beautiful landscape was all too infrequently seen as the prevailing weather in this part of the world and at this height was misty sheets of soft rain with visibility almost nil at times. Clear sunny days were a rarity. As I retraced my footsteps it was sad to leave the fanciful wonder of the heights for the reality of the valley below.

The Ubiquitous Sheep

If the mountain was in easy reach of the village, so was the village of easy access to sheep. In the summer, these ubiquitous animals were content to graze peacefully on the mountain slopes, but in late winter and early spring and especially when the new lambs started to arrive and the grass was in short supply, they were forced to seek sustenance elsewhere. They were small in size but exceedingly agile and could jump incredible heights. Being so active, they were very lean. Accordingly, Welsh lamb was very popular and in much demand. Their wool, however, was poor, thin and meagre in quality. Lowland sheep were much bigger and slower moving. Consequently, they carried much fat, but their wool was of excellent quality. Thomas Love Peacock wrote:

'The mountain sheep are sweeter
But the valley sheep is fatter
So we thought it meeter
To eat the latter'.

As I have said, in late winter and early spring, hunger would drive them to the streets of the valley below for sustenance. Favourite sources of supply were the buckets and boxes of rubbish left on the streets for collection by the refuse collectors. Coal was so cheap and plentiful, the miners' families kept huge fires even in the summer, which, of course, resulted in such a large amount of ashes that collections had to be made daily. When the sheep came down, the streets were deserted. Miners had gone to work and the families not yet up and about. There were no bins or bin liners in those days. The sheep would rummage in the rubbish until they had eaten their fill. They left the rest strewn all over the road to be cursed by the 'ashmen', as they were then called. People took great care to keep their garden gates shut or sheep would create havoc.

I don't know if the sheep had telepathic communication, but if they found some obdurate barrier, which defied all efforts to dislodge, down from the heights of the mountain would be summoned a huge ram, slow and majestic in approach and sporting a most impressive beard. With his armour-plated head, he would attack the object until it was dislodged. He would then, in an attitude of supreme condescension, stand aside and allow his harem to have first pickings.

George Phillips, who was a friend of ours, got up one morning and, opening his front door, was astounded to see a huge ram ruminating contentedly on his front lawn. He had consumed huge quantities of succulent grass, far more than could be found on the mountainside at that time of year. George, very annoyed, immediately started to drive the ram out, but the animal, panic stricken, instead of making for the open entrance gate, made a rapid short cut and attempted to jump over the surrounding railings. He failed miserably and hit the railings with his huge body so forcibly that he took the railings, together with the supporting pillar with him. What was once a trim lawn with a stout pillar was suddenly transformed into a mass of stones, bricks and railings. The ram speedily made off as if his life depended on it, leaving George staring unbelievingly at the havoc created. It involved him in considerable expense. He had to enlist the aid of the Council workers, firstly to place lamps around the heap of rubbish at night to prevent accidents and finally to restore the railings and pillar to their former condition. Poor George!

My mother-in-law's house was situated at the foot of the mountain slope, the valley being very narrow at this point. One day she went into the garden and inadvertently left the kitchen door open. When she returned a few minutes later, she was astounded to find a sheep and its lamb sitting comfortably in front of the fire. It took her all the work in the world to eject them. They were very loth to leave the warmth and comfort of the fire.

On another occasion, the door of her garden shed, where the vegetables were kept, was left open. On going into the shed, she met a sheep with a cauliflower in its mouth. She immediately gave chase to try and retrieve the vegetable, but the sheep speedily bolted with the cauliflower still in its mouth, through the side entrance on to the main road. A bus coming down the road had to swerve violently to avoid the animal. The bus driver, in a violent rage, stopped, opened the door and shouted, "You nearly caused a nasty accident and lives could have been lost and all because of a bloody cabbage!" My mother-in-law retired discomfited.

The ravages caused by the sheep aroused much friction between farmers and general public, but after many years of bitter and constant bickering, the mountain slopes were finally fenced in. Even then, some of the more agile sheep managed to find their way on to the roads. They were sometimes very hard to remove once they were settled sitting on the road, constituting a constant traffic hazard.

One day I was walking along the mountain slopes where a fence had been erected to keep the sheep out. As I walked along I could hear cries of distress coming from both a sheep and a lamb. When I reached the scene, I saw that a little lamb had burrowed its way under the fence and was trying unsuccessfully to get back. The ewe was running frantically inside the fence, almost mad with worry. I caught the lamb, which was very small, apparently only a few days old, and put it back over the fence. I expected the sheep to be overjoyed at the return of her loved one. But no! She was very angry! She butted the poor lamb all over the field. One could almost hear her saying, "Don't you ever do that again! You almost frightened me out of my life. Take that and that and that!" at every butt of the head, to the great astonishment and anguish of the poor lamb. However, her maternal feelings gradually returned and they were soon friends again.

Even in more modern times, sheep continued to be a nuisance. The road over the Bwlch Mountain dividing the Rhondda and Ogmore Valleys was long and steep. About half way up was a lay-by, which gave a magnificent view of the valley below where motorists often stopped to admire the prospect. Some motorists were misguided enough to give titbits of food to some of the sheep who had gathered curiously around. Those animals must have been expert gossips and soon the news spread round that a car in the lay-by meant food. From then on, motorists found it hazardous to park there. They would be surrounded by a huge flock of sheep expecting to be fed. They literally had to barge their way out.

In some spots, the road ran at a lower level than the mountainside and the sheep, heedless of oncoming traffic, upon jumping down would sometimes narrowly miss landing on the bonnet of a passing car. One can imagine the horror of the motorist to see a huge, shapeless mass hurtling down immediately before him

I have spent some time describing the antics of these animals, but they formed an integral part of our lives in those early days. They were ever present. Sheep and coal were the chief symbols of the valleys.

Weather and Wages

The town of Porth was about 200 feet above sea level and the surrounding hills were about 1100 feet, so it is not surprising that the Rhondda Valley boasted, if this is the word, the second highest rainfall in the whole country, surpassed only by the village of Seathwaite in the Lake District. The shelter of the surrounding hills meant that strong winds were rare, so that the rain fell in soft misty sheets across the valleys. Sometimes the mist was so low that the mountaintops were completely obscured and the valley below lay in a grey dim light all day.

If it was raining in the morning, the rain fell continuously all day. Indeed, sometimes it rained for days on end, which resulted in the river overflowing its banks and flooding the surrounding district. The trouble was accentuated by the fact that Porth was the confluence of the two Rhondda Rivers. Traffic was completely blocked and had to make long detours to reach its destination. I frequently encountered floods on my way home from school in the late afternoon, forcing me to take a longer route. Fortunately today, floods are largely things of the past because constant dredging of the riverbed with modern machinery has largely obviated the danger.

This damp climate, however, had its compensations. We were never short of water and periods of drought were unknown. As the rain fell on heavy clay and rocky soil, the resulting tap water was so soft in character that it did not take much soap to create an abundant lather for washing and shaving, and the drinking water was wholesome. In later years, after returning in the summer from a holiday in a hot, dry country, it was very refreshing to hear the patter of raindrops and feel cool water caressing your cheeks.

My father's wages as a coal mincr were but £2 a week and, looking back, it is a matter of great astonishment to me that he was able to raise a family consisting of a wife and five children on that meagre sum. But we never seemed to lack the essentials. We were adequately clothed and fed although our diet was unvaried and, no doubt, lacking in many essential vitamins. This is borne out by the fact that in a school photograph taken in 1911 we all looked very undersized compared with the young giants of today.

My father worked a 6-day week, Saturday being a working day and each day lasted 8 hours – 7 am to 3 p.m. He received his weekly wages at the end of the Saturday shift with the result that the main shopping had to be done on Saturday evening, the shops being allowed to stay open until 11 o'clock. In my very early days, wages were paid only once a fortnight, the non-paying Saturday being known as 'Saturday blank'. On that Saturday, I did not receive my usual pocket money of one penny and had to be content with an apple purchased from the visiting greengrocer's cart. There were no paid holidays in those days, and the only non-working days were the Bank Holidays, with, of course, no pay. What was therefore surprising was that my father was able to take the whole family for a week's holiday in the summer to our grandmother's house at Ferryside, during which he lost a week's wages. Sadly, we had to discontinue this holiday when our family got too big for my grandmother to cope.

The ravages of inflation are worthy of note when I say that my father's wages of £2 per week would be equivalent at the present day to about £200 per week. To give another example, I stated earlier that during the strike of 1926, I gave up all my salary to assist the family's income. My salary at that time was £13 per month, £2 of which I kept for my personal expenses. Every other Saturday, I went to Cardiff to see Cardiff City who were then in the First Division of the Football league, drawing crowds of about 25,000 for every match. My expenses for that day were as follows:

	£	s.	d.
Train fare to Cardiff		1	6
Admission to the match		1	0
High tea at the YMCA café		1	3
Theatre gallery seat			9
10 Player's cigarettes			6
Total		5	0

i.e. 5 shillings or 25p

Today, 25 pence is not enough to buy a newspaper. Therefore, I was able to get a day's entertainment in Cardiff for less than the price of a newspaper today.

When I got married in 1933, my salary was £24 a month and on that income we were quite comfortably off, lacking for nothing and being able to afford a lengthy holiday in the summer, often a month in duration, also a week's holiday at Easter. It has to be realised that this was done entirely on my income because women teachers were dismissed when they got married.

When in 1926 during the miners' strike, the authorities learned that I was an income earner supporting the family, they cancelled my father's unemployment pay of 17 shillings a week, called the 'dole'. Evidently, they believed in the old Victorian virtues that when a member of the family was in dire straits, the rest of the family should rally round and give help, a far cry from today when those distressed immediately have the aid of the State. Of course, there was no Welfare State in those days, but some form of aid did exist which was called Parish Relief. The main recipients of this were usually the widows of miners killed in the mines or the wives of disabled miners. An impression is that the relief given was very meagre. I do not know whether this body, the Board of Guardians, was nominated or elected, the former I suspect because I cannot recall any elections.

The women receiving Parish Relief generally supplemented it by casual or part time work, such as taking in washing or helping in domestic work for the better-off families. This was until such time as the young sons in the family grew up and were able to take up jobs to help their family. In this way, they managed to survive, but it was hard going.

A Load of Coal, White Lime and Shwni Wniwns

Coal, plentiful and near at hand, was comparatively cheap. There were two methods of delivery. The first was by a one-ton load delivered in a huge cart drawn by 2 horses, a shaft horse and a 'pull-up' horse which was only hitched on when they encountered a steep hill which they did quite frequently. During this operation, there was much shouting and sometimes cursing on the part of the haulier urging the horses to greater effort.

When the load arrived at its destination, the coal was simply unloaded onto the pavement outside the house, releasing huge clouds of dust. If the weather was windy, the result was calamitous. The load had to be carried to the coalhouse in the back yard. This task confronted the poor father when he arrived home, already tired from his labours in the mine. It was easier if the house had a side entrance, and in that respect we were lucky. However, if there were no side entrance, the coal had to be carried through the house to the yard. A huge task confronted the female members when they began to clear up after coal. This meant washing the floor on hands and knees with a bucket of water and a very hard brush.

My father strictly supervised storing of coal. Biggest lumps – and some were huge – were carried in first and placed in front to form a wall to prevent the rest of the coal from falling into the back yard. Behind these were thrown smaller lumps and on the very top of the pile was what we called 'small coal'. This was very fine, almost dust, and was used to bank the fire when it was not actually used for cooking or heating water. The male members then had to finish this Herculean task by throwing innumerable buckets of water over the back yard and pavement outside and then sweeping them with a very hard brush. We slept well that night! It was a hard life, but we survived which made us all the more ready to appreciate the few strokes of good fortune when they happened.

The second method of delivering coal was that used mainly by private coal merchants. It consisted of bringing the coal, already packed, in hundredweight sacks slung over the workmen's backs.

The job was quickly done and soon finished, but it was much dearer and was used by the better-off families who did not wish their houses soiled by coal dust. This was a method, which the miners could not afford.

The Valley humour is very pervasive and it even broke through this disagreeable task. The story goes that Dai The Coal Man had gone for a holiday in Paris and when he returned, he was anxious to air his French to show how clever he was.

Accordingly, when Mrs Jones asked him to deliver a load of coal to her house, he immediately replied, "Certainly, Mrs Jones. How do you want it? Cul de sac or al la carte?"

Street vendors were a rarity in those days. There was one old fellow who paraded the streets holding a basket of eggs in one hand and shouting "Fresh eggs! Fresh eggs!" But I never saw him sell any, eggs being considered a luxury and a trifling article of food. Miners demanded more substantial meals.

There was another character called Seth who was completely blind and owned a cart for carrying white lime. This was driven by a young lad with Seth walking behind, his hands on the tailboard for guidance. He cried in a loud, resonant voice, "White lime! White lime"! Lime, in great demand, was used to cover the walls of outside toilets, which required regular attention. As a boy, I was convinced that Seth's blindness was caused by the lime, whose dust naturally flew into the air when handled.

Seth's loud voice, with great carrying power, earned him another job, that of an unofficial town crier. He was employed by different collieries to announce the general meetings of their workmen. He was accompanied by a young lad carrying a bell and holding Seth's arm to guide him. They would halt at corners, the boy would ring the bell, and then Seth would announce the meeting. "A mass meeting of all workmen employed at the Cymmer colliery will be held at the Cymmer Workmen's Institute on Tuesday 25th March at 7.40 p.m. when important matters will be discussed. Please make every effort to attend". Then they would proceed to the next corner and repeat the performance.

Vendors who were very well liked were the French onion sellers (Shwni Wniwns – Johnny Onions) who came over every autumn, took lodgings and stayed the whole winter to sell their produce. They all lived near the town of St Pol de Lion in Brittany. They came around the houses on bicycles with the onions tied to the handlebars in long strings. Their onions were magnificent specimens, firm, well ripened and sizeable. They were reasonable in price and generally found a ready sale. The onion sellers were not pushing salesmen, but polite and unobtrusive, always willing to take no for an answer. They were always ready for a chat, several years here gave them a working knowledge of the language and they were always willing to talk about their families. They never seemed to go to England, but seemed to have an affinity with the Welsh people, for many of their place names, like those of Wales and, indeed, Cornwall, began with the prefix 'Tre' (town) and 'Pen' (top or end). They were all part of the Celtic races that were driven to the uttermost ends of their countries by the invading Saxons. Some spoke Welsh.

Another band of immigrants who came to this country to improve their lot were the Italians who had left the poverty stricken districts of their country. Unlike the French onion sellers, they were not migratory, they had come to stay. They opened a number of attractive cafes, very tastefully decorated, which gave much needed colour to the dingy streets of the Valley towns and were well supplied with all kinds of refreshment and confectionery. Oddly enough, they settled mainly in the mining districts of South Wales. The first Italian who came to stay was named Bracchi. The people of Wales pronounced the 'ch' as in Welsh, which sounded like a man clearing his throat. The success of the first Italians encouraged further people of their country to follow their example. They bore names like Bacchetta, Malvisi, Gamborini, but the Welsh people persisted in calling them all by the name of that first Italian, Bracchi. The Bacchetta brothers of the Station Café, Porth have performed a service in popularising Rhondda's local history in photographs, books and in a collection of early café equipment.

They were eager to succeed, working long hours, opening early and closing late. Being Catholics, their families were large in number, and all members worked with a will to make their venture a success. They were all very popular and well liked, very tolerant and easy going and did not mind if you stayed for the whole day on one item of purchase. Their premises were havens of warmth on cold winter nights, when other shops were closed, refuges of refreshing coolness in the height of summer. They were exceptionally busy on Christmas mornings when the young bloods of the area were eager to spend their extra pocket money and Christmas gift money and to smoke a surreptitious cigarette.

The Penny Rush

In the early days of my youth, Saturday morning saw me attending the 'Penny Rush', the weekly attendance at the Grand Cinema for the showing of the 'living pictures' as they were called. They seemed to be one of the wonders of the modern world. The name 'Grand Cinema' was a misnomer if there was one, for it was a shabby building, long and narrow, with no room to spare between the rows of seats, provided with only two exits in addition to the main entrance. If ever we were unfortunate enough to have an outbreak of fire, the consequences would have been horrendous.

The first few rows of seats had no arms so we would hear the usherette crying, "Sit closer. There's plenty of room", with the result that we spent the afternoon crushed closely together often against people of unwelcome odours.

The owner, George Roberts, was enthusiastic with a very baldhead and fresh complexion. Before the performance he would appear on the stage to entertain us. He would tell a few funny stories and, as it was the period of the First World War, would lead us in singing the National Anthems of Britain and France, finally to boo the Germans. He would also lead us in singing the comic songs of the time, silly songs like the following:

Hold your hand out, Germany
Hold your hand out, Germany
Britain and France will make you dance
Hold your hand out Germany

Or

The sun shines bright on Charlie Chaplin
His shoes are cracking
For the want of blacking
And his old baggy trousers needs a-mending
Before we send him
To the Dardanelles.

Why the Dardanelles I know not. We sang these songs with great gusto until our voices were hoarse.

Sometime, he would purchase at a very reduced price unsold copies of the comic papers like *Chips* and *Comic Cuts* awaiting shredding at the wholesale warehouses and would distribute them free of charge to his eager audience. They were very popularly received.

The programmes generally shown consisted of short feature films, a few comedies, with comedians like Charlie Chaplin and Buster Keaton in the infancy of their careers appearing in two part, knock about films often accompanied by the famous Keystone Cops. Their famous, longer films like 'The Gold Rush' were yet to come. By far the most popular films with the youngsters were the two part serial thrillers in which the hero, or more often the heroine, in their struggle with evil forces, survived the most dangerous hazards. At the end they came to a most exciting climax with the heroine in extreme danger of her life. Unfortunately, when tension was at its highest and almost too hard to bear, the film would end suddenly with the caption, 'To be continued next week', the announcement accompanied by shouts of dismay from disappointed youngsters.

The most popular actress was Pearl White who appeared in films like 'The Exploits of Elaine' or 'The Perils of Pauline'; or 'The Clutching Hand' in which a clutching hand appeared at the end about to seize the heroine. The excited youngsters, transfixed with terror, would shout, "Look behind you" with the film, as usual, ending suddenly with the promise that it would be continued the following week.

Most films were American, the British film industry being in its infancy, but I can remember the names of the principles who where Henry Edwards, Alma Taylor and Chrissie White.

As I got older, I began to find my weekly attendance at the cinema very boring. The noise of shouting, heat and close proximity put me off and my attendance became infrequent and I gave up. The Grand Cinema knew me no more. No longer did I sing that Pearl White was "Our Picture Queen" incessantly every Saturday morn.

The only other cinema in the town was 'The Rink', a more commodious building with a large entrance and exits so it did not present a fire hazard. The seating, again, was horrendous in the cheapest section consisting of hard, wooden seats. It did not hold any Saturday performances for children and did not attain the same popularity as the Grand, possibly because there was no one in charge with the charisma and enthusiasm of George Roberts.

In the centre of town was the Palace theatre, which presented plays and variety performances. I went there on several occasions with my father with tickets in the gallery, called 'The Gods' whose elevated position gave us a perfect view of the stage. The seating, as usual, was very poor consisting of wooden benches with no backs. At this, perhaps, we had little cause for complaint as the price of admission to the Gallery was but sixpence for adults and three pence for children.

We went there on three occasions, the first of which featured a play called the 'Royal Divorce' which depicted the divorce of Napoleon Bonaparte from Josephine Beauharnais so that he could marry Marie Louise of Austria. Only a youngster at that time, I found the play very heavy, but I was entranced by the resplendent uniforms of the men and the women's elegant dresses which added colour to the scene and presented a welcome change for our eyes.

I have hazy recollections of my second visit. It seemed to be a series of humorous sketches, some with a narrator which were unrelated to each other. One of them, I recall, showed a woman seated on the stage, obviously expecting someone, but was startled to see a sinister figure emerging from the wings, obviously a villain up to no good, twirling his pencil-like moustache as was the wont in those days in heavy melodrama, with the resonant voice of the narrator booming as the villain emerged from behind a tree and cried, "Behold! You are not alone for I am with you!" that is all I can remember of that scene.

The third of my visits was just as hazily recollected. A young man was standing alone on stage when there entered a figure entirely enclosed in a white sheet bearing a plate containing what appeared to be pieces of bread and butter. Indeed, it was so, because when the hooded figure cried, "Hamlet! I am thy father's ghost! Take away this bread and butter and bring me some toast." Very puerile, I thought, but the audience seemed to like it because they immediately broke out in raucous laughter.

On this third occasion, the theatre was crowded as the programme was much to the liking of the audience as it was greeted with a huge cheer. It presented three exhibition-boxing contests. Boxing at that time was very popular with the crowd and also with the boxers themselves for it gave them a welcome addition to their meagre earnings at the mine, especially if they won. The miners produced some excellent fighters because the hard work in the mines, hacking at the obdurate coalface, gave them muscular arms and terrific punching power.

In the first exhibition bout appeared Jimmy Wilde from Tylorstown in the Rhondda, a little man with matchstick arms and legs. He always looked as if he was in the middle of a serious illness, weighing no more than 7 stone with the result that he always had to fight opponents much heavier than him. However, he dispatched them all early in the bout with hammer-like blows from his powerful punches. Very few bouts went the whole duration and he remained unbeaten until late in his career when age took its toll. He was very popular at the headquarters of boxing, the National Sporting Club in London. They called him 'The Ghost with the Hammer'! Strangely enough, after his retirement he put on tremendous weight.

The second boxer was Jim Driscoll, an Irishman, born and domiciled in Cardiff. He was a featherweight, never weighing more than 9 stone. He was a very clever, skilful boxer which earned him the title of 'Jim the Peerless'. However, later in life, he became very ill and was a permanent invalid.

The third boxer, Frederick Hall Thomas, hailed from Pontypridd. He spent much of his time fighting in America, where he was called ''Freddy Welsh'. He was a lightweight, weighing no more than 10 stone, possessing neither the punch of Jimmy Wilde nor the skill of Jim Driscoll. He was, nevertheless, a tough all round boxer who became very popular in America and finally became Lightweight Champion of the World.

Many Americans in those days were very fond of capping their teeth with gold if they could afford it. Freddie Welsh, in his increasing prosperity won by his boxing skill, followed their example. In his bout at the Palace Theatre I could see his gold teeth shining in the stage footlights as he sat smiling in his corner.

It will, no doubt, be noticed that the three boxers were small men, like many Welshmen. The exhibition bouts they fought in the theatre lasted only 3 rounds compared with 20 rounds in real bouts in those days. The three boxers simply sparred with their opponents and no heavy blows were exchanged. Still, it was most entertaining.

Eventually, the theatre had to close as attendance gradually dwindled, people being lured by the greater attraction of the 'Living Pictures' in the cinemas. After it closed, it was bought by a company from Cardiff who made extensive alterations to the building and transformed it into a handsome edifice, tastefully decorated and comfortably seated which they called the Central Cinema. It proved very popular with the general public with the result that it soon overcame all competition from the Grand Cinema and the Rink which were ultimately forced to close down, relics from the past and soon forgotten!

What happened to George Roberts, you may well ask? George was his usual resourceful self and in no time at all became manager of a cinema in the neighbouring village called the Ynyshir Hall, a post he held for a number of years. But alas! Fate ultimately caught up with him. He was trudging home one night after the evening performance when he was waylaid at a dark corner by a gang who seized his bag containing the takings from the evening performance. They rapidly made off with a substantial sum of money, leaving poor George prostrate on the ground. They were never caught. This incident caused great consternation in the village because crimes of this nature were unknown there. The whole affair was too much for George, he resigned from his job and left the public scene. That crime was a rare blot on the town's escutcheon.

Head of the Household and Family

These incidents were but interludes in a very busy life. I have already described my father's arduous work in the mine. He arrived home about 3.30, tired and coal-dust covered and ate his meal immediately, too hungry to wait for his bath. By the time he had finished his meal, we had arrived from school. If the weather was fine, we went out to play, but if it rained we had to stay indoors and take refuge, all huddled together on the sofa in order to get out of the way while my father had his bath. This operation took place only at weekends because there was an age old superstition among the miners that too much washing weakened the back, a strong back being essential for the hard work of hacking at the coal face. Consequently, his back remained unwashed during most of the week, its washing taking place on Saturday. Imagine the state of his shirt and even the bedclothes. While he was on his knees beside the bath, we were careful to keep out of his way because if we moved, he would immediately shout, "Watch my feet! Don't tread on my feet!"

After he had washed his upper half, he let down his trousers and, quite naked, would step openly into the bath, modesty keeping his back turned away from us. After he had dressed, he helped my mother to empty the bath contents into the sink and disappeared upstairs for a short rest at which we all heaved a sigh of relief and got ready for tea.

My father was a very distant man and never condescended to play with us – perhaps he was too tired. He never physically chastised us, it was not necessary. His word was law and that was sufficient and, in any case, we were a very docile family of children and rarely, if ever, gave trouble. We were not exactly afraid of him, but we stood in great awe of him. In a male dominated society the husband brought home the money and kept order and the mother accepted this without question. Quite often did I see my mother take her baby in her arms, clasp his hands and sing:

Clap hands, clap hands
Till Daddy comes home,
Daddy's got money
And Mammy's got none.

It must be remembered, too, at that time, despite the efforts of Mrs Pankhurst and her followers, women had not yet obtained the vote.

My father was not on good terms with his in-laws. They never quarrelled for the simple reason that they were not on visiting terms although they lived quite near to each other. They had different life styles. My grandparents were a very happy family, content with their lot, extremely kind to those in need. They seemed comfortably off and lived accordingly. My father, on the other hand, looked at every penny twice before he spent it. Unlike my grandparents, he was never outwardly affectionate, but when we visited our grandparents' home which was often, we always received a warm welcome. My father had a sister, Eleanor, living near, but she was of a similar disposition to him, only more so. We never went to her house if we could avoid it. Oddly enough, she was very fond of my elder brother. He was the favourite and every Sunday, she insisted on his coming to tea, a visit that he hated and which he always tried his best to avoid. She was married twice, but had no children. Her second husband was John Owen, who had lost all his fingers on one hand, leaving only stumps from the first joint downwards. He endured all his wife's tantrums with equanimity. My aunt had an overwhelming fear of thunder. At the first clap of thunder, she would rush into the cwtch under the stairs and cover her head with a heavy coat so that she stood in complete darkness. Later she would emerge from her shelter, not one whit ashamed of her silly behaviour. She was certainly an odd character in many ways.

She was also very mean, she lived in the house built and formerly occupied by her parents before they retired to Ferryside. It was deemed hygienically wise to place the toilets as far as possible from the living quarters. Hence, the toilet in her house was located at the end of the garden, and as the garden was quite extensive, it took quite a walk to get there. On winter evenings, if my aunt received a 'call', she would turn down the gas to save that commodity which otherwise would keep on burning during her absence.

During one of my infrequent visits, she sent me all the way down to the main shopping centre in Porth to buy two rice cakes. I returned with two ice cakes. She was very angry and immediately sent me back to change them. Her anger was even greater when I returned to say that the shop assistant had refused this request because the condition of the cakes had suffered somewhat during the two journeys. She looked at me in distaste and cried, "You stupid little boy!"

Her English was not all that good. One day she sent me to the house of one of her neighbours, Mr Thomas, to borrow what she called a "stillion". This request astonished Mr Thomas who exclaimed, "A stillion? Never heard of it. Ask your aunt what she wants it for". I went back and returned with the answer "For weighing". He laughed and said, "She means a steelyard". And so it proved. I returned in triumph carrying the desired article, but not a word of thanks from my aunt.

Her English pronunciation, too, left something to be desired. She was in the habit of pronouncing her b's like p's. For example, bananas became 'pananas'. My father as a collier on the coalface was allowed to take home blocks of wood for firewood. Occasionally, he would give one to my aunt and when I took it to her, it would become a 'plock' of wood.

Then in 1926 occurred an event, which ultimately, after some vicissitudes, changed the course of her life for the better. When the miners returned to work, defeated after their six months' strike, John, her husband, like many others including my father, was dismissed. My father, an able bodied man, 52 years old, never worked again. Later in my life, I often wondered how hard he tried to find work as I, now being the only wage earner in the home, gave up the whole of my salary, except for a few pounds for personal expenses, to maintain the family. Poor John, some years older than my father and handicapped by his disabled hand, had no hope of finding employment. Consequently, he was nagged and harried by his wife, so much that he got desperate and together with a neighbour, Gomer Morgan, he decided to emmigrate to America. With a loan of a few hundred pounds from my father, John set off to cross the Atlantic, travelled across America and finally ended up in Los Angeles in California where he settled and found a job. At that time America welcomed immigrants, for there was an acute labour shortage. He seemed to prosper and in an incredibly short time he was able to send for my aunt. To the utter astonishment of us all, she went immediately, crossed the Atlantic, endured the rigours of the famous, or rather infamous, immigrant authorities of

Ellis Island, was met by John at New York and was soon settled in Los Angeles. America at that time was a land of opportunity, a 'get rich quick' country and if one worked hard and acted wisely, one prospered. This they did, invested their savings, they must have had expert advisers – and in no time at all they too prospered. It all sounded incredible.

In the late 1950s my aunt died and shortly afterwards John became ill. He soon showed signs of senile dementia and was taken to hospital where he lingered for a considerable time. He had become a fervent Chapel-goer and was regularly visited in hospital by his pastor, who knowing that John was now a man of considerable means, naturally wanted to know if he had made his will and to whom had he left his money. He was aghast when he learned that the legatees were his nephews and nieces in England. The thought must have come into his mind, "leaving money earned in America to a set of Limeys in England! No! Never!" He immediately set out to persuade poor John to alter his will. In this he succeeded at last, and the will decreed that the whole of John's estate should be given to the Church with the exception of a sum equal to the loan given to John my father when he left for America, plus accrued interest, to be left to his nephews and nieces in England. The accrued interest had been invested for some 30 years and was actually bigger than the original sum, leaving us with £230 each.

We immediately queried the will and asked our local solicitor to obtain a copy, which he did. After a thorough perusal of its contents he informed us that everything in it was quite legal and that we would be foolish to contest it. Reluctantly, we agreed and I took all the legatees by car to the Commissioner for Oaths, who lived in Mount Stuart Street in the heartland of Cardiff Docks. There the matter was finally settled and we each duly received our legacy.

I was very angry with the whole matter, for if my sisters had received their due share, it would have removed all their financial worries. When my father had died in 1954, he had left us each £110. I gave my share to my sisters, which aroused the ire of my elder brother who accused me of "showing off". But he kept his share nevertheless. I therefore kept my share the second time, about which later on I felt very guilty.

There was one other matter about this whole affair, which puzzled me. What on earth possessed my father to give John Owen the loan to finance him on his venture? My father was a very cautious man and it was entirely out of character for him to lend John that substantial sum, especially as he was out of work at the time and was convinced that John was venturing on a wild goose chase and that he would soon return with my father's loan totally dissipated.

Unlike his in-laws, my father, as I have indicated, was very parsimonious, rarely spending a penny on himself. He would visit local pubs very rarely. He was very saving and deducted only 2 shillings a week from his weekly wages of £2, out of which he would occasionally indulge himself with a packet of Woodbine cigarettes – 10 for 2 pence.

On Saturday night, pubs did a roaring trade. 'Roaring' was an apt description. They opened quietly at 6 o'clock, but gradually filled up until by the closing time, called 'Stop Tap', every room was full to the door with miners. One had to shout in the prevailing hubbub to make oneself heard. 'No women allowed' was an unwritten law which was just as well as the language frequently was too coarse for feminine ears. As the night wore on and the level of alcohol consumption rose, the noise became increasingly deafening, tempers got short and fights ensued. The fighters were ejected by the innkeeper and his bouncers, but nothing daunted, the fighters continued on the roadside outside. Sometimes they had to be stopped by the police who showed good humour and patience when they intervened. From their experience they well knew that it was only beer talking and that by the following morning, the cause of the fighting would be forgotten. Consequently they showed great tolerance. And they were right! The following morning all some of the fighters had to remind them of the events of the previous night was a sore head. Perhaps these weekly carousels did them good, they relaxed tensions and enabled them to forget for a short while the horrors and perils of the mine.

My father's drinking habits were infrequent and less boisterous. Sometimes he would meet an old friend whom he had not seen for a considerable time. They would repair to a neighbouring pub, take their seats in a quiet room where they would chat about old times, so interesting that they would forget how much beer they had drunk. Not being a regular heavy drinker, it was clear that he had over-indulged as he entered the house, stumbling over the doorstep. These occasions were very rare but every time they would terrify me.

He would stare vacantly about the room for a moment and then fall heavily into his chair, his usual, distant, unapproachable demeanour replaced by a maudlin, sentimentality. He would call me to him, smooth my cheeks, ruffle my hair and cry "My lovely boy, Ivor" while I stood before him, half in fear, half in disgust, sickened by the odour of his beer-laden breath. Sometimes he would be sick and vomit into a bucket in the scullery (which we called the lobby) filling the tiny room with fumes which seemed to percolate the house. At this juncture, my mother would have had enough and would bundle him unceremoniously upstairs to his bedroom, where he would fall into a drunken sleep. Women had a lot to put up with in those days. It was a very chastened father who presented himself the following morning.

A Woman's Place

Of all the members of the family, it was my mother who by far bore the heaviest burden. She was busy the whole day long. She had to provide four meals a day for herself and five children. She had to do an enormous amount of washing and ironing. She had to provide a meal for my father when he returned home from work during the late afternoon, help him in his bathing and then prepare for the children's homecoming from school, bath them all on Friday nights and ready them for bed. She must have heaved a sigh of relief as the last one disappeared up the stairs. And what of my father, you may well ask? Didn't he help? The thought never entered his head. In a male dominated society, it was considered demeaning for a man to descend to the menial jobs of the woman.

I had some inkling of the burdens borne by the women of the day, but I did not realise the full implication until later in my life. However, I did try to help and on Saturday mornings I would clean the back yard by throwing on it innumerable buckets of water and brushing it down with a hard brush. I would also don an apron, go down on my hands and knees and scrub the floor of the scullery, no easy task when one considers that the floor consisted of bare flagstones. I would implore my brothers and sisters not to reveal to my friends that I had descended so low in performing tasks usually done by women – I would have lost caste!

My mother and I were great friends. This was possibly due to the fact that, during my early childhood, I spent much time indoors with constant bronchial trouble. I lost time from school and seldom ventured outdoors during the cold weather in the winter. She treated me as a grown up and entrusted me with many confidences. Like a good daughter, she visited her parents at least twice a week, and it must have been a break for her away from the incessant work of the home. She welcomed the well furnished, spotlessly clean, comfortable surroundings of her former home, a startling contrast to the bare boned, utility of her own abode. This was always difficult to keep clean for any length of time because of our close proximity to the pithead and its coal dust. It was a constant struggle.

As my mother produced a new baby every two years, she was often with a baby in her arms during her visits to her parents. She always carried the baby in the shawl, Welsh fashion, that is with a huge shawl wrapped not only around the baby, but her own body as well so that it made the baby easy to carry and kept them both warm. In those days, it was unknown for a woman to venture forth into the open without some form of headgear so my mother, knowing a big hat commonly worn in those days would be cumbersome while holding a baby, would don my father's flat cap and sally forth thus attired to the great annoyance of her mother when she arrived. My grandmother, being a stickler for the conventions on more ceremonial occasions like going to Chapel or a concert, said it was simply not done for a woman to attend not wearing a pair of gloves. Skirts were worn ankle length, so it must have been very difficult to keep the hems clean during wet weather and its accompanying mud. Even a man would be looked at askance if he appeared without a flat cap or on more ceremonial occasions the inevitable bowler.

I have mentioned cleaning the back yard. A most amusing incident happened some years ago when Alan Whicker visited the area. In one interview, he came to Tylorstown and questioned a lad whom he met on how the lad spent his Saturdays and the following conversation ensued.

"Oh", said the boy, "in the afternoon, I go to the pictures during the penny rush and in the morning I clean my auntie's back". Whicker, "How long does that take?" Boy, "About an hour, sometime an hour and a half." Whicker, "Why does it take so long?" Boy, "Because after a week, her back gets very dirty." Whicker, "What do you use to wash her Back?" Boy, "A large number of buckets of water and a hard brush." Whicker, "Does it hurt her?" Boy, "How could it? She stands at the kitchen window watching to see if I am washing it clean." Whicker, "She stands at the window watching you clean her back?" Boy, "Yes."

Shop, Pop and the Co-op

In addition to cleaning the back yard and the lobby, I did a fair amount of shopping. Before the advent of Morgan Hicks' shop in the next street, we did our grocery shopping at the shop of William Rees, which was situated in the main street of Cymmer and therefore not far away. The shop was run by William and his wife and was quite adequate for our requirements. There was a kind of family connection because my Aunt Martha worked there as a nanny cum housemaid and slept in except for weekends. They had six children, three boys and three girls. The boys, as they grew up took jobs in the shop. Mrs Rees also helped, but had the habit of putting h's in her sentences when not needed and leaving them out when they were. She would greet you with "Well, h'Ivor, h'any h'eggs today?" and, "'ow is your mother? Is she quite well?"

The miners' financial situation improved considerably during the First World War. Welsh steam coal, being of the finest quality, was in great demand and much sought after by the Admiralty to supply the ships of the Royal Navy. The miners, therefore, were able to obtain higher wages, but it was of little avail in raising their standard of life. As their money increased, the supply of food declined, not only in amount, but also quality. As in the Second World War, the German U-boats wrought havoc among the ships of the Merchant Navy.

Ever lengthening queues for food became common and caused considerable ill feeling. It was a case of survival of the fittest, which often meant the richest. The big food companies were able, by means of their resources, to obtain larger supplies of food then their smaller counterparts. Poor William Rees with his one shop had no hope and his customers suffered accordingly. We were obliged to queue outside the larger shops to amplify our supplies. The call would come "Margarine in the Maypole", rush down to queue outside their shop, "jam in the Home and Colonial", similar procedure. And so it went on. It was almost a full time job!

Not only the amount, but the quality of food declined. Butter disappeared and was replaced by a margarine, dark brown in colour, not nice to look at and not nice to the taste. The recognised brands of jam fell out of supply, replaced by a kind of jam, which looked as if it was not made of fruit, but of swedes. White sugar disappeared without trace and in its place appeared a sugar, dark brown in colour, which made tea look like liquid mud. White flour was no more and instead we had a flour, very grey in colour, which lacked the bright whiteness of the usual flour. A shop loaf made of the same flour was called 'a standard loaf'. Our staple diet seemed to be grey bread with brown margarine, washed down often by sugarless tea. Meat was also in short supply and we had to make do with what we could scrounge from the butcher.

Anti-German feeling ran very high during the First World War, but in the Rhondda there were very few Germans upon whom this anger could be vented. However, there was a jeweller's cum watch-making shop in the main street of Porth owned by two Germans named Ruf and Kalten Bach. They were inoffensive people who would have continued to live in peace had they been left alone. But a wave of ill feeling against them was aroused and fomented by Mrs Watts Morgan, the wife of the sitting Labour MP. One evening, she headed a gang of people and made such inflammatory speeches outside the shop that the enraged crowd smashed the shop

Station Street. Note Welsh Hills, Thomas & Evans on the awning

windows, broke into it and completely wrecked the premises. That was the end of Ruf and Kalten Bach! The premises were boarded up and were never to be seen again.

The biggest and most successful grocer's shop in Porth was Thomas and Evans, founded by two Welshmen. Thomas sold out early leaving William Evans sole owner. The firm was very successful and opened branches on the outskirts of town that were called Terry stores. William Evans was even ambitious enough to manufacture his own brand of tea, which was called 'TevnaTea', a play on the two names Thomas and Evans. He was very sympathetic to the cause of the miners and during their many strikes, he allowed them to run up huge debts and waited with patience for them to repay when the strikes ended.

But outside the Rhondda, he was best known for his soft drinks bearing such thirst-quenching names as American Cream Soda, Dandelion and Burdock, Limeade, etc. Not only did he have a wholesale trade with shops, but his delivery men also visited individual houses, selling cases containing four large bottles of 'pop' as it was popularly known, at the price of 6d per case, or 1½ pence per bottle.

William Evans

(from 'William Evans' by Owen Vernon Jones)

They were delivered during the early days by cart, but later with the advent of mechanised traffic, by lorries. These vehicles having to be serviced and maintained in a serviceable condition, a garage and paint shop were built in the town at the bottom of Cymmer Hill. My youngest brother, Trevor, who showed little academic ability, was employed in the paint shop and worked there all his life.

A factory to manufacture the drinks was built on the riverside adjoining the colliery yard and the factory workers consisted mainly of a band of tough girls from the streets named Lincoln, Argyll and Brook Streets. In those days, no self-respecting family would dream of allowing their daughters to work in factories. Usually the young female population would be employed in domestic service, or as shop assistants, or if they had obtained a little extra education in the higher grade school after leaving the primary school, as clerks.

The villages of Glynfach (Little Valley) and Cymmer (a confluence) were separated by a brook, which flowed down the mountainside. In its initial stages, it was a clear, lovely, limpid stream, but when it reached the environs of the three aforementioned streets, which bordered its banks, it became a turgid mass of slimy water, littered with matter of all kinds thrown in by the inhabitants. These included bodies of cats and dogs, ashes, cardboard boxes, old mattresses and sticks of discarded furniture. Rubbish lay rotting for days until provident showers of heavy rain would carry it downstream, past Glynfach whose steep slopes of the narrow valley called the Cwm (narrow valley) conveniently hid it from sight, past the colliery to be reluctantly received by the river, reluctant because it already had its own load of rubbish to contend with, mostly slurry and colliery waste from the pits higher up.

These three streets were no go areas and no boy from Glynfach would dare enter unless accompanied by an adult. Alone he would be set upon. Sometimes, this ill feeling would break into open warfare with each side throwing stones from opposite sides of the brook. The enemy would have a slight advantage, their bank being higher than ours. However, we must have all been inexpert throwers because I cannot recall any instance of a boy being hit.

Sometimes, after I had entered the Grammar School, I would encounter these factory girls on their way home from work as their homeward journey passed the bottom of our street. I dreaded these encounters. They would gather around me, jeering and shouting terms of abuse as I pushed past them, "County Snob!" the 'County'

Bronwydd
(from 'William Evans' by Owen Vernon Jones)

being the name given to my school, try to snatch my school cap and if they thought that I showed unnecessary force in pushing past, would shout, "Coward! Hitting girls! Wait till we tell our brothers!" a threat not to be ignored as their male counterparts were only too willing to bear a grudge.

Another tough bunch was the boys from Top Trebanog, but they were quite friendly and not inimical to strangers. Their ebullient spirits were manifestations of rude health, engendered by living in fresh air untainted by coal dust.

The firm of Thomas and Evans continued to flourish, both in the grocers' business and the soft drinks trade, despite the tendency of Williams Evans to give extended credit to the miners' families during their many strikes. Indeed, his prosperity was such that in a rare, unspoilt corner of Porth, he was able to build for himself a magnificent mansion house which was called Bronwydd (Goose's Breast).

He had no children, and his will stipulated that after his wife's death the house should be bequeathed to the District council. It became their Treasurer's department. Later I visited there one day on business and it was gratifying to hear cheerful cries of "Hullo, Mr Howells," from the clerks who were mostly old pupils of the County School. William Evans took a great interest in the County School and in his will he left a sum of money for a Trust Fund to establish 6 prizes, 3 for boys and 3 for girls. He also donated the first fire engine and first public library to Porth.

Eventually, William Evans died, and after his death a Board of Directors was formed who soon succumbed to the blandishments of a firm called Beachams who took over and bought the soft drinks section. The grocer's section remained unsold as no firm could see any prospects in a shabby valley town continually beset by strikes. Accordingly, the main shop in the middle of town, as well as the outlying Terry stores, were closed, causing many redundancies. My young brother kept his because he was employed in the drinks section.

I may as well complete the story of Bronwydd. This unspoilt corner of Porth was transformed into a public park, donated by William Evans, boasting a swimming pool, two tennis courts and a bowling green, together with a band stand in which, as far as I know, no band has ever played. Thus, in the Rhondda amenities were added and conditions improved.

Now came an item of news, which to us was somewhat startling. At least, it seemed startling to us because it was so unusual. My father announced to us that the Ferndale Co-operative Society had established a branch in the town of Ferndale, a small town about five miles away, whose picturesque name belied its appearance. "You see", said my father as we could nearly hear him smacking his lips in anticipation, "You see, we would all become shareholders and if we clear all our debts by the end of the quarter we would receive a dividend (the Valley people pronounced it 'davidend') which would mean that profits would go not to people like Thomas and Evans, but back to us." It seemed too good to be believed, and my father seized the opportunity with open arms.

But it was not my father who had to endure the consequences of this development, but my poor mother as usual. Every Saturday morning she had to travel to Ferndale to do the shopping. The only means of transport was by the mastodon of the past, the electric tram. A tram under way would sway from side to side like a ship in a gale. If you were brave enough to take a seat in the upper deck, you would take your life in your hands. You would be thrown about and it would take the expertise of a Wild West cowboy on a bucking bronco to maintain his seat. The tramcar ran on rails and was connected to the power lines above by a flexible rod with a little wheel at the end.

Tramcar bound for Porth

Sometimes this rod would become disconnected – not surprising in such a rough journey – and would have to be reconnected by the poor conductor, a job not easy at any time, but very difficult in the dark. Bad language flew through the air, and the poor conductor was not helped by the plentiful but unwanted advice from a crowd of onlookers who seemed to materialise from nowhere.

The driver's lot, too, was not an easy one for he had to drive through the day standing on his feet, but it always seemed to me when I saw a tram approaching that he was too tall for the job as his vision appeared to be half-obscured by the destination board directly above his head.

Later on, a further branch of the Co-op was established at Pontygwaith which eased my mother's burden because it halved the length of the journey. When I had finished my housework on Saturday morning, I would go down to Porth square to meet my mother and I would carry the heavy burden of shopping up the steep slope of Cymmer Hill.

This state of affairs continued for about 2 years when the inevitable disaster happened – inevitable because, sooner or later, it was bound to happen – but it was a blessing in disguise for me and especially my mother. The Society became bankrupt! This development was only to be expected because, first of all, few of the dividend holders bothered to vote in the annual elections to the Committee who controlled affairs. Consequently, the Committee became a close corporation. Corruption was rife and supervision over the assistants was nil with the consequence that they stole at will.

This was not the end of the story. An enterprising estate agent with an office in Tylorstown, some people would call it enterprising, but I would call it unscrupulous and hard-hearted, bought the whole debt from the Society – I didn't know that this could be done. He immediately started to dun the dividend holders for payment of their debts. At first, the holders were unperturbed as they were under the impression that their dividends covered their debts. But no! This was not so, the dividends not having yet been paid were counted as assets and all assets had disappeared in the payment of debts to avoid bankruptcy. Luckily, my father with his carefulness always paid 'on the nail' as soon as the goods were purchased and, therefore had no debts outstanding, so we were spared visits from the debt collectors. There was great rejoicing among all members of the family that visits to the dreaded Co-op were over. The only exception was my father who saw his dreams of prosperity vanish into thin air. 'The best laid schemes o' mice an' men gang aft a-gley'.

And where were we going to shop now that the Co-op was no more? Who would come to help us? The answer was easy. Who else, but good old Morgan Hicks who had just opened his new shop in the street adjoining ours? Our shopping troubles were over!

Handymen and Women

It was a strange feature of Valley life that few bothered to cultivate their back gardens which were adequate in size and which could have produced a supply of fresh vegetables – welcome addition to our monotonous diet. Perhaps the reason was just lack of spare time, the miners' only free day was Sunday and that in many cases was spent in regular Chapel going, or perhaps it was pure tiredness. After a hard day's work in the mine, few miners would be inclined to resume similar work in the evenings. Their main requirement was rest, which was perfectly understandable. Of course, growing flowers was out of the question! One cannot eat flowers!

My father was no handy man. The only extra job he would undertake was minor repairs to the boys' boots which consisted mainly of knocking in little nails which we called 'sprigs' and studs, and the whole operation was called 'tapping' which, indeed, that was really what it was.

For this operation, extensive preparations had to be made. My father would sit down in front of the fireside armed with a last, a box of sprigs and a hammer. Soon sounds of tapping could be heard in the air, only to be interrupted by a yell of pain. My father had hit his finger instead of a sprig. We were very careful to keep out of the way on these occasions. After the job was finished, more or less to his satisfaction, he would stand up, dust his clothes and explain quite seriously to me, "You see, Ivor, to do a proper job, you've got to have the proper tools," which presumably he did not have, hence the botched job. To that I could have added "And it would be useful if we had a proper handy man," but I refrained, discretion was the better part of valour.

My Uncle Bob, on the other hand, was a true handy man who could turn his hand to practically anything. When I was a boy, he cut my hair regularly at the behest of my grandmother and he even gave me my first shave with what was called a 'cut-throat' razor, which could be a hazardous operation in inexpert hands. He hailed from Pwllheli, in North Wales, worked in the mine, and lodged with my grandmother for a short while before marrying my Auntie Martha, my mother's youngest sister. After marriage, they settled to live two doors away from my grandmother. He took over an allotment, which produced an abundant supply of fresh vegetables for the family, but none percolated down to the Howells family because of the strained relationship which existed between my father and his in-laws. They must have thought, "If he wants vegetables, let him grow some." On the other hand, when we visited them, we were amply rewarded.

The women of the time seemed to be more versatile than the men or perhaps they were prepared to work harder. Some did domestic service for the better-off families in the area. Some took in washing, others became part-time shop assistants, especially at weekends. In every village, there was one woman, getting on in years, who took on the job of 'laying out the dead', generally assisted by a younger woman who was 'learning the trade'. In those days there were no Chapels of Rest, no embalming, the undertaker's task simply being to measure the body and supply the coffin. The body was conveniently placed on trestle tables in a spare room, in our case, the parlour.

Valley humour is ubiquitous and even penetrated into these macabre situations. The story is told of one incident, of two layers preparing a body for burial. The elder woman had completed the job of washing and was looking for underclothes to begin the task of clothing the body ready for burial when the younger woman said, "I will go to fetch the clothes hanging on the line in the garden", when the elder cried frantically, "Oh no! Don't do that! I haven't aired them yet!"

In another story, Dai had just died and his closest friend, Tom, had come to view the body and pay his respects. Standing beside the bereaved wife, "Poor old Dai," said he, "he looks very well too". "Yes" replied the wife, "that week he spent in Porthcawl in the summer did him the world of good".

But the funeral itself was observed with the greatest respect. The men, bowler-hatted, dark suited and black shod would gather discreetly some distance away from the bereaved house where the Minister was hold a funeral service with near relatives, the bier and the coffin having been quietly delivered some time before. There was no funeral hearse or carriages for the mourners. We simply could not afford them. The men mourners had taken a day off from work, which meant losing a day's pay. At a discreet signal from the undertaker, the men would gather outside the house whilst the coffin was brought out, borne on a bier. Led by the Minister, they would sing an appropriate hymn. The miners' rough voices would gradually blend into a smooth crescendo whose liquid notes lingered long in the air and in one's memory. The men sang with feeling and fervour for were they not singing a last farewell to a fond friend with whom they had faced, uncomplaining, the many perils of the mine?

And so the sad cortege moved slowly on like a sluggish stream bound on its last journey, down the steep slope of Cymmer Hill whose incline made it very difficult for the coffin bearers, each step having to be carefully taken to synchronise with those of his fellow bearers, down into Porth square, turn left at the tramway depot, treading delicately over the tramway rails, so difficult to negotiate, then up the long, steady climb of Cemetery Road, before finally arriving at the gates of the cemetery, a distance of about 1 1/2 miles of laborious journeying. The cemetery was simply a part of the mountainside with a steady climb from the bottom to the top.

When we arrived at the grave side with the grave already prepared, there was a short final funeral service begun by the Minister with a few appropriate words of condolence and concluded with a repeat of that glorious singing, but even more impressive as the sound of the voices rose in the pure air of the mountain side. Then the mourners slowly wended their weary way homewards, back to the life of hard reality which awaited them, another chapter closed.

Women showed their usual versatility, even in the art of paper hanging. Painting the house was usually done by the man when he could spare the time supplemented by help from the women. A professional painter and paperhanger, we simply could not afford but paper hanging was for the expert, and in every village there was one woman who had the expertise. In our village, our expert was Annie Prosser.

Our father's parsimony showed itself only too plainly in the condition of the house's decoration. The bedrooms were not papered, but covered with a kind of green paint wash, whose colour never changed during my life in that house. The same fate befell the lobby, which remained green, except that it was constantly renewed as it was in continual use. The parlour had been papered, but only once. It was never used because in the winter we could not afford an extra fire and summer was spent as far as possible out of doors.

Only the kitchen received regular paper hanging, always a great event. First of all, Annie Prosser had to be consulted as to her availability, she being in great demand. Then a book of patterns was obtained from the paint shop and many were the committee meetings held in our house between my mother and her friends before the final choice.

Then, at last, the great day arrived! We were packed off to school as early as possible. When we returned for our lunch, a scene of great disorder greeted our eyes. The only article of furniture which occupied its original position was the table which was the main scene of operations, all others were pushed to corners of the room and covered in white sheets. My mother's head and that of Annie Prosser were protected by a kind of white turban and their faces covered with white splashes of paste. We were despatched back to school as quickly as possible after lunch hurriedly taken. When we returned from afternoon school, we found the kitchen transformed into a place of beauty. Annie Prosser had gone, her work completed, leaving my mother in proud possession of a transformed kitchen. Every wall was covered by beautiful new wallpaper. It was a miracle and we simply could not believe our eyes! My mother was a very proud woman that day!

Another regular visitor, because he was very necessary, was the chimney sweep. Our sweep was a mineworker engaged on the night shift. Those night workers who complete five nights' work were regarded as having done six nights and paid accordingly, presumably because they were regarded as unsociable hours. It was not particularly arduous work like working on the coalface and was generally performed by the older worker.

Our sweep arrived on Saturday mornings which, being the end of his working week, suited him admirably. He brought the tools of his trade with him, a large number of sacks, a circular brush, and a series of rods which, when fitted together would prove as tall as the highest chimney.

The rods were connected together with the brush at the top. All exits from the kitchen were covered with huge sheets of sacking to prevent soot from escaping. All the young males of the house were despatched to the back garden to inform the sweep when he had finally broken through. They would shout in chorus to the sweep,

"You are through! You are through!" at which the sweep, pleased at this welcome news, would give a triumphant twirl to the brush in happy acknowledgement, pull down the brush and the rod with its attendant load of soot. The amount of soot was almost beyond belief. The sweep would then pack up the load and carry it out to his handcart. He was so expert that no soot was visible on the fireplace. Was it a trick of the imagination, or did the fire really burn more brightly after the operation?

It seems as if I was a great favourite with my maternal grandparents from the very beginning. I did not know whether it was because I was small and delicate in health that they called me "little shrimp" but I gradually came to believe that it was because I was rather advanced for my years, they said that I had "an old head on young shoulders" and that they were very amused at what they termed my "quaint sayings". In fact, we became so attached that I began to call them "Mum" and "Dad", much to the annoyance of my real father who took me aside one day and said, "*I* am your father, *I* am your dad. Your grandfather is Tommy John's dad, and your grandmother Tommy John's Mam." Tommy John was, of course, their son. And so it was! My real father had said so. An apostrophe 's' was outside the limits of my vocabulary at that time. They became known to me as "Tommy John Dad" and "Tommy John Mam." If I went to visit them, I would say, "I am going to see Tommy John Mam," and so it remained during my early years.

Gradually and unobtrusively, especially over the weekends, I did become a member of my grandparents' family. It happened so gradually that no one seemed to notice it, at least no comment was ever passed. It simply happened!

On Saturday evenings, I accompanied my grandmother on her weekly shopping expedition to the town centre in Porth and helped to carry home her many purchases. It has to be remembered that at that time there was no means of public transport between Cymmer and the town centre. It was a stiff climb uphill all the way back and had to be done on foot. Still, I always thoroughly enjoyed the evening because when all purchases had been completed, we repaired to the shop of the Misses Howell (no 's' and no relation) who, amongst other things, made delicious faggots hot, steaming and most acceptable on a cold winter's night. They were very popular. We sat at a small table where my grandmother was able to rest her weary limbs while I wolfed down the faggots. The two spinsters also made toffee (which we called 'taffee'), of which my grandmother made ample purchase so that I could take some home and share it with my brothers and sisters. Thus refreshed both in mind and limb, we would begin the long trek up hill and homewards!

I spent the whole of every Sunday in my grandmother's house. The summer mornings were spent in the allotment, recently taken over by my grandmother's lodger, Bob Jones, who was later to become the youngest daughter Martha's husband. The allotment proved a great success and produced a large variety of vegetables, a welcome addition to our menu. The allotment also had many blackberry bushes with ample supplies of delicious fruit.

Our Sunday meals were a great advance on our usual Spartan fare at Blosse Terrace. We had an extra vegetable in addition to the 'taters and meat'. We also had 'afters' of a rice pudding or some blackberry or apple tart. Sunday tea was also a delicious meal consisting of jelly and blancmange, or tinned fruit and custard. An unwritten law of this meal was that you had to eat some bread and butter before you were allowed to partake of its 'afters' – no bread and butter, no afters! The rule was always strictly observed.

Winter Sunday mornings were spent reading the Sunday newspaper. My grandparents' reading material had improved greatly in standard during the years. Instead of the *Police News* with its lurid tales and blood-curdling pictures, they now took the *News of the World*, which was a great improvement?

To resume my Sunday story, I was sent to Sunday School in the afternoon and taken to Sunday Chapel in the evening.

My bond with my grandparents' family grew ever closer. One day, my Aunt Nannie came to visit her parents. She was my mother's younger sister. She had recently married Theo James who hailed from Tylorstown higher up the Valley. He was employed as a haulier at the colliery at Llanbradach, a mining village in one of the adjoining valleys and lived in two rooms in the main street. She was a very cheerful person, always ready to see a joke and easy to get on with. Her husband, Theo, was of a similar disposition.

During this visit, it was decided that I should go and spend a week with them at Llanbradach. I don't really know the reason for this, but I suspect that my aunt was very lonely. A newcomer to the area, she had not been able to form any lasting friendship, while my Uncle Theo, also eager to make friends spent many evenings at the local men's club.

And so it was decided and so I went. I found Llanbradach smaller and even dingier than Porth and my aunt's two rooms were so small that it gave little space to move about. They were situated behind a small grocer's shop in the main street and entrance was effected by a passage at the side of the shop.

I have just mentioned that my Uncle Theo was a haulier. The road along which he had to travel with the pony and trams of coal were very rough and uneven and consequently the rails were very roughly laid and it was not uncommon for the trams to come off the rails. To lift it back with the front part of your body was to invite a permanent hernia. So the haulier found it easier to hoist the trams back on the rails with their hands clasped behind their back giving it a good heave. To minimise the contact of the haulier's back against the hard side of the tram, a square of tough, thick leather, called the 'pisyn tyn' was provided by the colliery and tied in front of the haulier's waist. 'Pisyn' was, of course the Welsh word for 'piece' and 'tyn' the vulgar word for one's posterior. The pieces of leather were, no doubt, made to measure because the hauliers like everyone else, came in different sizes.

A Holiday in Trefechan

As time went on, my relations with my grandparents grew ever closer. Every few years, they would spend a holiday in Aberystwyth in order to visit their place of origin, Penryn Coch, which was only a few miles away and in which some of their relatives still lived. They always took me with them.

Aberystwyth means the mouth of the River Ystwyth and if ever there was a misnomer, this was one. The mouth of the River Ystwyth was at Tan y Bwlch, a few miles down the coast to the south. It was an undistinguished river flowing through flat, featureless country and meeting a quiet, uneventful end among the level sand dunes of Tan y Bwlch.

It was an arduous journey by train to Aberystwyth. At least, the route chosen by my grandparents was. The shorter route was the Great Western Railway necessitating only two changes at Briton Ferry and Carmarthen, but my grandparents always chose the northern route which was much longer and during which we had to change at Pontypridd, Merthyr, Ponsticill and finally a two and a half hour wait at Moat Lane Junction to catch the Shrewsbury-Aberystwyth train. My grandparents were adamant and told me that that was the route they had always taken. Despite my urgent protestations that was the route they were going to take on that day too. So Mr Smarty Boots had to hold his peace.

Trefechan was our destination where we finally arrived hot and tired. My heart sank when I viewed the promised land. My Uncle George and Aunt Mary lived in a small, dingy cottage, at the very end of a similar row of buildings. To my great surprise, both my uncle and aunt spoke with an English accent and there was some vague talk of their having lived in Manchester during a part of their lives. Uncle George had just retired, he had a florid complexion, a large red nose and a white moustache. My aunt, on the other hand, was a tiny, wizened woman with wrinkled features and small eyes which she kept blinking as if she had just awakened and was trying to find her way which was not surprising for her living room seemed to be in permanent semi-darkness and harboured a foetid smell as if the windows were never opened. I shudder to think what conditions were like at the rear of the house. My aunt had a quiet voice, hardly louder than a whisper. Uncle George, on the other hand, was a garrulous man and never seemed to stop talking.

But this place was full of surprises. To my delight I found that they owned a small-detached cottage, a few yards away from their living quarters and entirely separate which they let out to visitors in the summer months. It had two rooms up and two down. It was clean and adequately furnished. It had a series of stone steps rising from the street below with iron railings, which enclosed a small front garden. This was our holiday home, which we found quite satisfactory. I might add that the cottage called Pant Cottage was the last house in Trefechan and the road running past it led directly into the country.

After a day to recover from our train journey, we set out for Penrhyn Coch, a distance of about eleven and a half miles, not a very pleasant journey in the hot sunshine on white dusty roads – tarmacadam was of the future. When we arrived, I found that the village consisted of a few cottages grouped around a small square and other cottages dotted here and there in the surrounding countryside. Aunt Peggy's cottage was on one side of this small square.

It was very tiny, with just two rooms down and two bedrooms upstairs. All rooms were sparsely furnished. Some furniture appeared to be home made, unpainted and very rustic looking. It was evident from the very beginning that my grandmother and Aunt Peggy did not see eye to eye on many things and while there was not open warfare, one felt that there was a campaign of hostility waged continually in their conversation, and it was not difficult to find the reason. One only had to note the smart appearance of my grandmother, very spick and span and beautifully dressed in startling contrast to poor Aunt Peggy with her rustic clothes and bedraggled appearance. My grandmother's disapproving looks as she glanced around her spoke volumes.

While the women talked, my grandfather took me for a short walk and showed me the cottage where they lived prior to their emigration to the Rhondda. It was in ruins, a heap of stones lying beside a small brook. My mother was a small child when they left and the sight of the ruined cottage brought memories for my grandfather who look very sad to see all that remained of his former house.

As there was no evidence of a man about the house, I assumed correctly that Aunt Peggy was a widow and lived alone. She had three children, a son and two daughters. The son, Will, was employed as a groom cum handyman at the neighbouring estate called Nant yr Eos (Nightingale's Brook). He apparently lived in for we never saw him. During his early years, there was some vague talk of his becoming a jockey.

The two daughters, Bet and Polly, had emigrated to the Rhondda, to live with their Uncle William and Aunt Mary at Pontygwaith. Uncle Williams owned a man's hairdressing business in the main street and the two girls were employed by him, Bet to assist in household duties as Aunt Mary was not taking kindly to old age, and Polly to serve in the shop which usually accompanied a men's hairdressing business. Uncle William was a cheerful, friendly man who for some reason which I never found out, was known to his clients and the neighbourhood in general as "The Terrible Turk".

I remember being invited together with my Uncle Tom, my mother's brother, to tea one Sunday. One item at this meal was rhubarb tart and I recall Uncle William, whose command of English was not of the highest standard, saying to me, "Now, come on Ivor, eat plenty of the rhubarb tart. Proper thing to break your 'thirsty'." This was our one and only visit to my uncle and aunt. Our paths never seemed to cross and I never saw them again.

Before our next visit to Penrhyn Coch a few years later, my grandmother complained that she found the walk from Bow Street to the village rather too much for her ageing limbs so it was decided that any other visits should be taken by horse and trap driven by my Uncle Tom who was adolescent and had acquired some driving experience by consorting with the sons of William Rees, the grocer. One will recall that my Aunt Martha was employed by Mrs Rees as a nanny cum housemaid and a close relationship had been established between the two families.

In Trefechan lived a lady, Mari Parry, who owned a small fleet of horses and traps, which she let out for hire. She was also the owner of a brake pulled by four horses with which, in the summer, she ran afternoon trips for visitors to beauty spots and places of interest like Devil's Bridge and Clarach. However, these excursions were not for us as one had to climb a few steps to get your seat on the brake.

Furthermore, when you arrived at a steep hill, you had to descend from your seat and walk because a loaded brake on the hill was too much for the horses. It was obviously a trip for the young.

We faced this journey to Penrhyn Coch with some apprehension, fully justified by events. First of all, we had some difficulty with the horse who, evidently, found Uncle Tom's driving hard to follow. However, the horse settled down and we arrived at Penrhyn Coch without incident. The difficulty was to find a stable for the horse. Aunt Peggy gave instructions, which were hard to follow. Uncle Tom unsaddled the horse and led him to the stable door which, when opened, revealed to our great consternation, a family at table busily eating their midday meal. However, they took it in good part and after a hearty laugh, directed us to the stable, which was quite near.

We thought our troubles were over. But no, there was more to come when, after our visit to Aunt Peggy's came to an end, Uncle Tom duly saddled the horse, took the animal by the head and leading him forward found that he had left the cart behind! The horse, no doubt, had come to terms with Uncle Tom's style of driving and we arrived home safely. He must have had many a hearty laugh with his fellow horses.

Some time later, my Aunt Martha was taken seriously ill and had to give up her job with Rees the grocer. It was thought that she was heading for a decline, which was Valley language for T.B. This disease was rife at that time and seemed to run in families. It was an illness lasting for years and usually resulted in an equally lingering death. Antibiotics were yet to come. Miraculously, after a few months' rest, she started to improve and it was decided that to complete the cure, she should spend a fortnight's holiday at Aberystwyth accompanied by the inevitable Ivor.

Uncle George was overjoyed to see us as at last, he had someone with whom to talk and listen to his interminable chatter. Aunt Martha was a quiet woman, softly spoken and very forbearing, but even she found Uncle George's talk hard to bear. He took us for long walks from which it was very hard to escape. I was very bored so in order to avoid monotony, I used to take a book or comic paper with me and as they would walk very slowly, I would race ahead, and finding a comfortable spot, would sit and read until they caught up with me. I would then repeat the performance many times until we had finished the walk.

We seemed to have arrived at Aberystwyth in the middle of a crisis of an affair of the heart. Uncle George and Aunt Mary had two male relatives whose exact relationship was very hard to determine. First there was Georgie, a young man in his early twenties living with them who was very lame and who earned his living repairing shoes in a small shop in the front room of one of the neighbouring cottages.

Living next door to them was another relation, George William, a man of about 50 years of age, with greying hair, a bachelor who worked in the local gas works, a very silent individual whom I never heard speak a word. He lived alone and had a daily woman to see to the chores. She was a spinster of about the same age and there was intense speculation among the neighbours as to whether they would get married. But in the shadows lurked another woman who had her eye on the marriage stakes, but whose chances of success were dismissed as negligible by the local gossips. However, just prior to our arrival on the scene, it was announced that he had just proposed to the less favoured of the candidates, the quiet one on the shadows. Loud and fierce were the recriminations of the rejected one and we had arrived in the middle of this. How did I, a mere lad, come to know about this sequence of events? Simply because I kept by eyes and ears open.

However, all in all, we thoroughly enjoyed our holiday at Aberystwyth. We had learned how to escape the clutches of Uncle George and as the weather was fine, we spent most of the time on the beach, Aunt Martha sitting comfortably in a deck chair while I busied myself playing in the sand or paddling in the sea. Consequently my aunt returned from her holiday much improved in health. Indeed, the improvement seemed to be permanent because shortly afterward she married Uncle Bob and lived in a house next door but one to my grandparents. All's well that ends well!

Christmas in Porth

In my early years, I found Christmas particularly depressing. All the shops were beautifully and attractively decorated, but at home there was nothing! We could not afford to buy even the most meagre decoration. The idea of sending Christmas cards never entered our heads and the cost, if we knew it, would have staggered us. There were no fairy grottoes in Porth shops where Father Christmas took little children on his knees to ascertain their wishes for Christmas gifts. We had to take whatever we found in our stockings on Christmas morning.

Some time before Christmas, we would gather together in little groups to sing Christmas carols on neighbour's doorsteps in the hope of a few pennies. After going through our repertoire, we would finish by singing the following ditty:

Christmas is coming, the goose is getting fat
Please put a penny in my old box hat.
If you haven't got a penny, a ha'penny will do,
If you haven't got a ha'penny, God bless you.

Needless to say, rewards were few, mostly nil, and truth to tell, we did not deserve any. Our singing was very poor, very ragged and out of tune. A similar fate met those who sang at our doorstep – the door remained resolutely closed.

Christmas was a particularly busy time for our poor mother. First of all, the Christmas cake had to be made and taken to the bake house to be cooked. Then followed the Christmas puddings, a most arduous time consuming and to my mind, dangerous task. They were placed in individual basins and put in boiling water in a huge boiler on a blazing coal fire. As the water gradually evaporated, the boiler was replenished with buckets of boiling water. I often wondered whether the whole operation was worthwhile.

On Christmas Eve, before we went to bed in a fever of expectancy, our stockings, duly labelled, were hung on an improvised line in the kitchen. On Christmas morning, we awoke early and our eldest brother, Will, was sent downstairs to fetch the stockings because we were afraid that we might meet Father Christmas still on his rounds. Brother Will had long had doubts about the existence of this generous, fabled being. Loud and fierce were the arguments about the matter and when our parents' opinion was sought, they upraided poor Will for harbouring doubts, but Will, though thoroughly discomfited, still remained unconvinced.

In the half-light of a cold winter's morning, we eagerly examined the contents of the stockings when they were brought up. The modern child would have broken into contemptuous laughter to see what we called our Christmas gifts. Our stockings were generally full of coloured paper to make them look more attractive and contained some sweets, nuts, an apple and an orange and beside them, duly labelled, was our one and only Christmas toy, only one, but nevertheless duly prized and appreciated. The apples were of a variety called Morgan Sweets. Sweets were a real misnomer because they tasted more like raw swedes, while the oranges, an import from Spain were small and bitter tasting. Varieties of apples and oranges like Cox's Orange Pippins, Gold Delicious and Jaffas were unknown to us.

At about eight o'clock while we were still in bed, our parents never getting up early on Christmas mornings, appeared what I appreciated greatly, the band of the Salvation Army playing Christmas carols at the corner of our street. They played for about half an hour, going through their whole repertoire before moving on to their next stop. My favourite was 'Silent Night, Holy Night' in which I pictured in my mind the moon shining in a dark blue, icy sky over a sleeping, snow-filled landscape – quiet silence, tranquillity everywhere with a feeling at the back of my mind that this peace would be disrupted at any moment by some unexpected disaster. Perhaps it was a reflection of the state of uncertainty which always prevailed in the minds of those living in a mining area, and yet, at the same time, such is the perversity of human nature, I derived a certain quiet satisfaction from the whole picture.

Our Christmas dinner was a big improvement on our usual main meals as we had an extra vegetable added. The meat was usually a joint of beef or a leg of lamb, a goose or turkey was too expensive – we could not afford such a luxury! We also had an unusual addition to the meal in the shape of our mother's Christmas pudding, which we thought delicious.

In the afternoon, we played with our new toys out of doors if fine, but as we lived in Wales, it was usually wet at Christmas time so that most days we had to play indoors.

There we were then, adults and children all confined to one small room. We simply could not afford a fire in the lounge, which we called the parlour. Soon squabbles arose between the children and our parents, longing for an afternoon's rest, became very irritable. We got on each others' nerves and the atmosphere was electrically charged. Darkness sets in early so our parents were glad to take advantage of this circumstance to give us supper and pack us off to an early bed. Thus peace was restored, much to the relief of our parents, another Christmas Day was over!

New Year's Day, on the other hand, was exciting. Strangely enough, the weather was usually dry and bright as if the Gods wished to make amends for the usual bad Christmas weather and wanted to start the New Year in good style. It was the custom for the young male adolescents to gather in small gangs and besiege the shops, shouting, "Please give us a New Year's gift." The shopkeepers fully recognised this custom and duly obliged, in their own way. In order to tease the youngsters and drive them into a frenzy, they would delay their action for as long as possible. At last, they would relent and throw out gifts to the excited crowd. The fruiterer would throw out fruit, the sweet shops toffees and chocolates, the confectioners cakes and biscuits, each shop was visited in turn. The boys arranged themselves in couples, a forager and a minder. The forager would dive into the scrum when the gifts were thrown, collect as many as possible and hand them to the minder to guard. In the end, we would have collected a considerable booty, which we took home to share with the rest of the family. Quite an eventful day was New Year's Day and a profitable one to boot!

Religion

At first glance, it would appear that Chapel played a large and important part in our lives. This impression was purely illusory. The people of the mining valleys had been over the years largely Anglicised while Chapel, on the other hand, remained stubbornly monoglot Welsh. The language heard spoken in the street was almost totally English, especially among the younger generation. Spoken Welsh was rarely heard and then only from the older generation.

I seemed to know more Welsh than the average youngster and the reason for this may have been my four-month stay at Ferryside. There I heard much Welsh for the people were bilingual, although their English was slightly accented, their vowels being shorter than ours. It is well known that the human mind in early days is very absorbent. Knowledge gained during early years remains forever in memory. However, my Welsh was purely conversational, the language of the hearth, the language of every day. Literary Welsh of books, the Bible and of the pulpit was well beyond my capacity and of most of my generation. It was ironic to hear people on the way to service speaking English only to listen to a sermon entirely in Welsh.

Every Sunday afternoon, we went to Sunday School. The school was divided by sex and age into separate classes. Each class was supervised by a teacher and ours was under the direction of Mr Windsor James, a deacon, by profession an insurance agent who we all suspected probably with truth had become a prominent member of the Chapel only to establish contacts to increase his business. The first part of the lesson was devoted to idle chatter among the boys who were all a little older than I, a recital of amorous conquests of the previous week, probably fictitious. Then Windsor James would bestir himself from his daydreaming or most probably from his next week's planning. He would ask us all in turn to read a few verses from the Bible, not a word of which we understood, then, knowing that we would all be asked to recite a verse from the

Bible to the entire school before it ended, we would hurriedly search for the shortest verse we could find, 'Duw cariad yw – God is love', 'Cofiwch gwraig Lot – Remember Lot's wife', 'Un duw sydd – There is only one God', being the favourites. When our turn came, the superintendent (yr Arolygwr) when he realised the brevity of our offerings, would say, "Da iawn – Very good", but the look in her eyes was venomous. If looks could kill, we would all be dead. Then after the collection of our few pence for the afternoon's offerings, we would sing a hymn and that signified the end of our week's Sunday School.

The evening service lasted about two and a half hours. First we would sing a hymn, then the Minister or preacher, as we called him, would read a chapter from the Bible. Then another hymn followed by the most important part of the service, the preacher's sermon that would last, at least, half an hour. The preacher would read a verse from the Bible and would explain every word, now and again lapsing into English to ensure that the explanation was fully understood. He was a small man with a musical voice and extravagant gestures, a member of the Bardic circle with the Bardic title of 'Pelidros' so that his full nomenclature was 'Y Parch W R Pelidros Jones', 'Parch' being the Welsh for 'Reverend'.

After about a half-hour of quiet explanation, the congregation would settle down to await the 'Hwyl'. This word has no exact English translation. The preacher's voice would gradually rise into a crescendo of eloquence, his brow covered with beads of sweat, his jowls slavering with intense emotion, his arms flung upward in confession of his sins, then lowered almost to the ground as he contritely begged for forgiveness. The regular Chapelgoer would listen impassively because he had heard it so many times before. But to the newcomer, it would present an astounding revelation. The Minister's tirade would be accompanied by shouts of encouragement and support from the more pious members of the congregation as the torrent of words poured forth from the Minister's lips. Then suddenly he would stop, look wildly about him and wiping the sweat from his forehead, would sit for a few moments in the pulpit in apparent prayer and quiet contemplation. The congregation would sit quietly waiting for him to recover from his eloquence, moving, impressive, inspiring and almost frightening in its intensity. Then he would rise and quietly announce the last hymn of the evening, which the congregation, inspired by the

Minister's sermon, would sing with the fervour of which only Welsh choirs are capable.

Our Chapel Pisgah was Baptist in religion where baptisement was total immersion. My eldest brother and my Uncle Tom had already been baptised and the Elders of the Church now considered that I had reached the age when I should seriously consider following their example. When I asked why I should do so, their answers did not satisfy me and I refused. Their reply was that baptism would wash my sins away. When I answered that, as far as I knew, I had committed no sin which would justify such washing away, they replied that I was born in sin, but they had no answer to my query as to how I could sin before birth. I was appalled at their answers to all my further questions, too numerous to be mentioned here, that, thoroughly disillusioned, I kept on refusing until at last they gave up, convinced that I had lost my soul to the Devil.

I really could not be expected to observe the vows they wanted to take before baptism, 'peidiwch a smygu' – 'do not smoke', 'peidiwch a yfed' – 'do not take alcoholic drinks'. They even required me not to go to "the living pictures" as we called the cinema. For example, they had learnt that Windsor James, one of the Deacons who was fond of the good things in life, had been seen going to the Central Cinema in Porth. Headed by the Minister, a deputation of Deacons visited Windsor to warn him to mend his ways. The wily old rascal did so, but not in the way they intended. He simply changed his place of entertainment. Instead of going to the cinema in Porth, he simply went to the cinemas at Tonypandy or Pontypridd where he was not likely to be seen.

I now go back a little to my story. The successor to Pelidros was a man whose name I have completely forgotten, so little impact did he have on my memory. He lacked the vibrant personality and lively manner of his predecessor and gave the impression that he had become a minister of religion simply because he lacked the ability, or perhaps the energy, to adopt any other career. Slow in speech and movement, he completely lacked the eloquence of Pelidros. Gone were the lively pictures, the metaphors and similes that graced the sermons of his predecessor and he frequently lapsed into English to make his meaning clear. One of his rare pictures was delivered in English, speaking of some misdemeanour or other, he would exclaim "I would never descend to such depths, I would rather crawl on my hands and knees over broken bottles all the way from

Land's End to John o' Groats." These words caused much secret mirth among his congregation who laughed inwardly at the picture of this poor man on his perilous journey, pausing to look for the next signpost to ascertain how much further he had to go. The Valley penchant for nicknames soon came into operation and henceforward he was known as "Broken Bottles".

He was a single man, much younger than Pelidros and lodged with Daniel Lewis, a pious man, at least outwardly so. Daniel had a daughter named Selina whom, as was inevitable, the Minister married. The atmosphere in that house must have been extremely pious for Daniel also had a son, Dewi Emlyn by name, who was a few years my junior in the Grammar School and who later became a Minister himself at Hopkinstown, a little village further down the Valley.

The Minister was allowed sabbatical leave for four Sundays during the year when he would either be invited to preach at other Chapels which would increase his somewhat miserly stipend or he would take a rest. I can imagine Pelidros being in great demand, but not his successor. On the Sundays during their absence, prayer meetings would be held, prayers being offered by the elders of the Church, and when one considers that their full-time education terminated when they were twelve years of age, the quality of their offerings was truly incredible. They would get down on their knees before the congregation and for about the space of fifteen minutes, their prayers would pour forth in a never-ending stream which sometimes made me wonder whether or not they were inspired by some outside force which, in turn, made me question and doubt my youthful agnostic tendencies. Between each prayer, of course, we sang a hymn.

Once a year, we held what we called "big meetings" which was a literal translation of the Welsh "cwrddau mawr" to which we invited two not one, of the most prominent preachers of the day. As these special meetings lasted well over two hours with a congregation likely to be increased by worshippers from other Chapels, it was politic to advise parents not to bring young children to the service. The special preachers, past masters in their art, would bring along with them their favourite sermon to deliver to a congregation seething in expectation. In their sermon, delivered with verve and passion, they so played on our emotions that at the end, we sat exhausted. Our hearts and minds were drained of all feeling as this was oratory of the highest order delivered by consummate actors.

Once a year the Chapel gave a tea to the members of the Sunday School. It was held in the vestry where trestle tables were laid out, one of which was occupied by the women of the Chapel busily preparing the meal. It always puzzled me that having divested themselves of their outer clothes and put on aprons, they retained their hats and kept them on their heads throughout the meal. When I asked them why, they had no satisfactory answer. Indeed, they looked puzzled as to why I had asked such a question and simply said that was the way they always did it and that was the end of the matter. The men of the Chapel played their part too, providing hot water for the tea in a boiler in the outhouse.

It was a simple meal consisting only of bread and butter and also cake of which there were three kinds, seed cake which I detested, plain cake which we now call Madeira and currant cake. The young people had a hearty meal and when it was all finished, the boys would indulge in a little boasting as to how many cups of tea they had drunk. "How many cups of tea did you drink?", "Six", "I can beat that, I drank seven". I refused to take part in this contest if it really was one, for knowing the boys concerned, I had my doubts. I saw no purpose in over-filling myself with liquid, which I had to let out later, sometimes at inopportune moments, so I took no part in these contests.

Barry Island - 1910

(Glamorgan Record Office)

Once a year an event took place, much coveted and anticipated by the children, but often reviled by the parents – the annual pilgrimage to the seaside at Barry. All the Chapels in the town would apply to the Education Authority for a day's holiday so that they could book a train for the whole contingent – a request always readily granted. My mother would get up at 5.30 to make all preparations for there was a lot to be done. My father never accompanied us on this excursion. Perhaps he thought that a day in the mine would be more restful than a day with a crowd of excited children, but I suspect that the real reason was that he did not want to lose a day's pay.

Our day began early. First of all, we were sent to the Chapel vestry to collect our railway tickets from one of the deacons – tickets which were not really needed for when we arrived at the station, no one bothered to look at them.

At the station, there was pandemonium, children rushing up and down the platform, children shouting, carriage doors slamming, mothers looking wildly about to ensure that all their broods were safely aboard. At last, we were off. The children behaved during the journey. There was much to engage attention. Rushing to the windows, they were able to view familiar landmarks from an unusual angle. "Ooh! Look! There's the Church! There's the pop factory! There's the river!" and when we left the confines of the valley, we saw unfamiliar landscape with eyes of interest, green fields dotted with neat farmhouses and cattle grazing quietly – a startling contrast to the bar, rocky slopes of our native valley. Arriving at Barry Station, the train quickly decanted its passengers eager for the beach, Whitmore Bay. It was eminently suited for children, extensive, with firm yellow sand and safe bathing. The surface had a slight slope so that one had to go far out before getting out of depth.

Inevitably, one of the children would fall in the water and spend the rest of the day running about in underclothes whilst his clothes were placed on rocks to dry. Inevitably too one would fall among the rocks and cut a finger or leg, which would necessitate the help of the St John's Ambulance. One would get lost and had to be retrieved from the lost and found compound. One would drop his sandwiches in the sand and would be forced to eat gritty food, grumbling all the while or he would drop his bottle of drink among the rocks and would be forced to carry the pieces to the nearest rubbish bin, again with many complaints. We were lucky in that we never had a wet day. I tremble to think what would have happened if it rained. Where would we have shelter? How would we pass the time?

The journey home was a nightmare. Children were tired, hot, irritable and quarrelsome. It was difficult to keep the peace. We finally arrived home and my mother, with a huge sigh of relief, was able to pack us all of to bed. She would say, "This is the last time! No more!" But come the next year, she would get up early in the morning to make preparations once again.

For myself, I was gradually getting more and more disenchanted with this outing so that when I went to Grammar School, I was glad of the excuse that the school did not have a holiday on that day. I was content to remain with school friends, happily eating my banana sandwiches with a swig of water from the tap.

On Tuesday nights in winter, I regularly attended the Band of Hope – where we practised for the annual singing festival. The Gymanfu Ganu was held every Easter Monday together with the other Baptist Chapels of the area at the parent Chapel Salem in the heart of the town. The children in the afternoon and adults in the evening, the singing on both occasions was glorious. The children's voices in the afternoon session pure and clear, while in the evening, the tenor and bass voices of the men choristers provided harmonious base for the soprano trilling of the women.

Held on Easter Monday, the women greeted the occasion by appearing in their Easter bonnets and new dresses, a scene so aptly described by Thomas Hardy in his short poem called 'Weathers'. I quote 'And maids come forth sprig muslin drest'. We listened eagerly to hear the song of the cuckoo that though a rascal of a bird, too lazy to rear its young, was, nevertheless, always warmly welcomed as a harbinger of the spring. When on the hillsides we heard him we would rejoice and sing the following ditty:

The cuckoo comes in April
Sings a song in May
Plays a tune in the middle of June
And then he flies away.

One year, following the festival, someone had a brilliant idea. Why not continue our Tuesday practices during the summer to prepare for a concert in the early Autumn? The takings could be used to replenish the coffers of the Chapel Treasury which were always low because Pisgah was a small Chapel and its members were few. We were aiming at a variety concert for all tastes. So it was agreed and practices began.

One of the items proposed was a playlet about which we had the gravest doubts, being novices in this business of acting. After some weeks of practising, it was decided to hold a rehearsal in the Chapel vestry before a selected audience of Chapel members. One of the principal actors was David Lewis, owner of the Penny Bazaar on the outskirts of town, the forerunner of the modern-day Woolworth's in that no article was sold above the price of one penny. Although, again like Woolworth, he did not always live up to his promises.

David was a real wag and could never resist a joke. Playing the part of John, one of the principal actors, he was saying goodbye to his friends, as he was about to immigrate to Australia, having been out of work for a considerable time. "Goodbye, Mrs Jones". "Goodbye, John and good luck". "Goodbye, Mrs Davies". "Goodbye John, I hope that you will do well", and so on to his friends on stage. Having completed his farewells, he turned and made his way disconsolately to the wings. There, he stopped, turned round, made his way back to the front of the stage and said to the puzzled audience, "And goodbye to you all", at which everybody burst into hysterical bursts of laughter.

In another scene, news had come that John had died suddenly in Australia and his widow was on the stage with her friends mourning his loss. "And he was such a good man and so nice looking," said she looking up at his portrait, which was not a portrait at all, but a rough drawing, drawn up hurriedly because the real portrait was not to hand. The drawing was so grotesque, that on looking up at it, she could not resist breaking out into peals of loud laughter and this being infectious, the rest of the actors could not help following. Further action was postponed until they had all recovered but it was alright on the night. Of course, the real portrait was produced and John ceased his antics.

We had a little chorus of young girls dressed in sailor's clothes, whether homespun or hired, signing a series of nautical songs. I can remember one:

Jack ahoy! You're the boy,
You're the boy we all adore.
You like to be on the rolling sea.
And you're just at home on shore.

Also we had a group of youngsters singing a nonsense song, a piece of doggerel which went as follows:

Coymee nayro, kiltokayro
Coymee nayro coymee.
Pimstrim, stamaddle, larrabone a rinctinc
Arignum, bullidim a coymee.

But the 'piece de resistance' was a little operetta entitled 'Helen'. A line ran as follows: "On the wall above the chamber where sweet Helen dreams at night". This word 'chamber' mystified the younger elements of the choir. Only one chamber did they know and that was the one under the bed. How could Helen? Accordingly, when they came to the line in practice, they sang, "On the wall above the chamber where sweet Helen *pees* at night". "Stop! Stop!" cried the presenter, "that's a strange way to pronounce the word 'dreams'. I don't seem to hear the 'm' sound correctly. Say 'm' together". We duly obliged. "Now try again". In the next effort, some of the culprits sang it correctly, but others didn't. "That's better", said the leader, "but not quite right yet. Let's try again". This time we all sang it correctly. "That's better," said the leader, "why didn't you do it like that before?"

This continued in like fashion for a matter of four or five weeks to the growing anger and mystification of the leader, wondering what had got into his stupid choristers. Then, one day, suddenly, the truth struck him. His wrath was wonderful to behold. We listened impassively, for we knew quite well that he would be unable to fulfil his terrible threats. Then in the middle of his tirade, the funny side of the affair struck him. The picture of Helen and the chamber was too much for him. The Valley sense of humour asserted itself and he laughed with us. "Now," said he, "you've had your little joke, now let's get on with some serious business". And so we did. No more fooling. Like the concert, the operetta was a great success!

But this was a 'one-off' affair. Practising for both the singing festival and a concert was too much for us, especially as our numbers were so few. Yet we had the satisfaction of knowing that we could do it and the Chapel Treasury coffers benefited considerably.

My usual habitat on Sunday evenings after Chapel was my grandmother's house, literally a stone's throw away. As I got older,

I became increasingly disenchanted because I was the only male present and I found the female chatter rather irksome. However, one summer evening on my way from Chapel, I met Ernie Manns, a boy slightly older who lived nearby, but was not a member of the Pisgah. He said, "Ivor, we're going for a walk to Ton (i.e. Tonyrefail). Would you like to come with us? I was only too ready to accept, so hurriedly informing my people where I was going, we set off. The walk to Tonyrefail, which was about three miles away, involved a steep ascent to Trebanog and an equally steep descent down to Ton. When we finally arrived there after a little larking about, as boys of that age are wont to do, we came across a motor car, which had broken down. Motor cars of that time were continually breaking down. Inside the car was a man who turned out to be the local doctor and who informed us that he had an important appointment later in the evening. We acted as the Good Samaritans and volunteered to push the car with the doctor at the wheel to his home. After strenuous effort, much puffing and blowing because Tonyrefail was as hilly as any Valley village, we arrived at our destination. He was very grateful, thanked us profusely and gave us a shilling each. Riches indeed!

The job done, we realised to our alarm that it was already dark. Not one of us was old enough to possess a watch. We set off hurriedly for home and when we arrived, we found the whole village in a frenzy, parents frantically searching for their lost ones, imagining all sorts of dire happenings, broken limbs, death, kidnappings, which kept racing through their minds. The village Bobby had been informed, but he, knowing boys, was completely unperturbed. Said he, "They'll come back when they are hungry".

The parents' anger turned to relief when they realised that we were unharmed and, what is more, they were mollified, even proud when they learned that our late return was due to the performance of a good deed.

I have endeavoured to depict for you the brighter side of religion as practised by Pisgah, but there was a darker side in which in pursuing the straight and narrow path, all enjoyment in life was to be eschewed and all pleasures of the flesh abandoned. It was, in fact, fundamentalism at the highest level. Baptism, which involved total immersion, washed all sins away, although what sins one had committee by this time of early adolescence passes my comprehension. Whatever misdemeanours one had committed by that age were mere peccadilloes involved in the process of growing up. Their religion was restrictive in all ways. One must not smoke – and that was before it was discovered that smoking injured one's health – because it was an indulgence of the flesh. One must not drink alcohol – my grandfather's supper consisted of bread and cheese and a glass of beer so a scout had to be posted on the doorstep while he consumed this harmless repast in case the preacher arrived unexpectedly and caught him out committing this dreadful sin. My grandmother was fond of an occasional glass of stout and had to give the wine stores strict orders to deliver the case of bottles at the side entrance to the house in order not to be seen. One must not enter a public house or the cinema, both haunts of the Devil.

Children must not be allowed to play their usual games on a Sunday, or sing comic songs. "Stop that whistling Ivor. Don't you know what day it is? It's the Sabbath". Sunday had to be devoted solely to attendance at the Chapel to worship, although I never understood why singing hymns and listening to the preacher could be called worshipping. All life on earth should be spent in preparation for that glorious life in heaven and it often occurred to me that surely it would be better to have only one life and that would be the life in Heaven transposed to earth. During my adolescence all these questions ran unceasingly through my mind and no one could answer them to my satisfaction.

Early School Days

Cymmer Infants' and Cymmer Junior Schools
1909 – 1916

I became a pupil at the Cymmer Infants' School in September 1909 at the age of five. Due to ill health, I was not able to start at an earlier age. I have a very hazy recollection of my stay there. The only feature that I clearly remember was that we were taught to read by the phonic method. I cannot even remember the names of all the staff. The head teacher, Miss Jones, had grey hair and therefore looked very old to my infant eyes; brown, wrinkled and unfeminine features with unwanted grey hairs sprouting from her chin. Altogether, she did not present a very prepossessing appearance. She was always dressed in black. I can also remember Miss Davies of the braying monotonous voice and a teacher called Miss Nellie who was my favourite. She was small and petite, bright and cheerful, always spick and span. She used to wear a snow-white blouse in the sleeve of which she kept a tiny, equally white, handkerchief, a habit, which for some reason fascinated me. I can

A typical Rhondda school c. 1913

also recall that there were four classes in the school – little babies, big babies, second and first classes.

It was in the infants' school that I received the only caning in my school life. I was a very docile pupil and always eager to learn. I was punished for a misdemeanour, which I did not commit. It happened in this way. Adjacent to the school building was a huge garden belonging to Ben the gardener who sold his vegetables and soft fruit much more cheaply and in fresher condition than the shops. One playtime, leaning over the garden wall, which separated school and garden, I watched Ben working and I was so fascinated that I lost all count of time. At last, looking round, I saw the playground completely deserted not a soul in sight. Thereupon I wrongly concluded that it was home time and proceeded to make my way home, calling as usual at my grandmother's house, which was situated quite near the school. Surprised to see me arrive so

Rhondda Junior School 1913

early, she promptly marched me back to school and left me there. Miss Davies, worried at my sudden disappearance, was very angry and gave me two strokes of the cane on the palms of my hands. These stung me and gave me great pain, but sheer indignation at this illdeserved punishment kept my tears at bay. I was determined not to cry. I never forgave Miss Davies!

Next, I became a pupil at the Cymmer Junior School. As the population of the district had increased tremendously during recent years by the influx of people seeking work in the coalfields, the school building could not accommodate the growing school population. Temporary buildings had to be erected in the school grounds pending the building of a new school and recourse had to be made to the use of vestries in the local chapels.

The headmaster was Mr Dan Jones, a well-known likeable man who exercised firm discipline by kindly methods. There were 6 standards or classes, the leaving age at that time being 13 years. Standard One was taught by Miss Edith Morgan, who had an overbearing personality and was not generally liked. She was a cousin of the headmaster and later became a head teacher herself in a neighbouring school. This Standard was taught in one of the chapel vestries.

The teacher of Standard 2 was Mr Leonard J B White. He was an Englishman with a distinctive English accent, foreign to Valley ears. We all tried to mimic him when he was out of ear shot. He was distant and supercilious and gave the impression that he found teaching a great bore. However, he was a good teacher, and we seemed to make good progress under his tuition.

Standard 3 was taught in one of the chapel vestries by Mr Rees Jenkins, a heavy and black-moustached man; a tormentor of little boys, heartily disliked and feared. We all hated him. Even the slightest misdemeanour was met by the words: "Go to the cloakroom and take your trousers down and I shall deal with you". The victim always returned in tears, but I don't think that he was corporally punished. I took great care not to offend.

The Standard 4 teacher was Mr Thomas Williams who was a native of the place and was called "Tommy Teacher". He was uncertificated, not having been to college, but he was an excellent teacher and we all made good progress. He was well liked and very popular.

Standard 5 was in the charge of Mr. Gomer Evans, dashing, swift of movement and smooth of tongue. He was very unfortunate to teach his class in the assembly hall under the watchful eye of the headmaster, who because of the overcrowded nature of the school had been forced to allow his private room to be used for other purposes. The headmaster in his turn had to do his work amid the constant hubbub of a class in full session. It was difficult to determine who was the worse off. Mr Evans later became the head teacher of a neighbouring school.

The instruction on the whole was thorough and comprehensive. At the end of every year we had a written examination in every subject, even handwriting and drawing, now called art. A report was then sent home to parents. There was no nonsense like the modern day trendy teaching in mixed ability classes. The only difference in the class in those days was age. If you did not reach the required standard, you were kept back in the same class until you did.

The first lesson in the morning was scripture, in which selected passages from the Bible were read. The following lesson was arithmetic, the first part of which was devoted to chanting tables. Next came a few minutes of mental arithmetic, and the major part of the lesson was given up to written arithmetic. After the playtime interval we had English, the first part of which was devoted to spelling, in which each pupil had to spell a word given to him by the teacher; then reading, in which each pupil had to stand in turn to read aloud. I cannot remember any pupil who could not read after such thorough practice. In the afternoon we had singing in which we were taught sol-fa, history, geography, Welsh, drawing, drill in the yard if fine and in the classroom if wet.

Some of the teaching was by rote. In geography, for example, we would recite the names of the rivers starting in the north with Tyne, Wear, Tees – I can remember them all now, many years later. We would then proceed along the coast of England and Wales until we reached the Solway Firth on the opposite coast. We were given sketch maps of England and Wales on which, after some tuition, we had to mark the principal towns. We knew that Ben Nevis was the highest mountain in the United Kingdom, Snowdon the highest in Wales and Scafell in the Lake District the highest in England.

In Welsh, we were given charts depicting everyday scenes with sentences in Welsh describing what was happening, e.g. Y mae Idris yn chwarae pel-droed – Idris is playing football. *Question* A ydy'r eneth yn chwarae pel droed? *Answer* Nac ydy, dydy'r eneth ddim yn chwarae pel droed. Similar sentences were: Y mae yr eneth yn chwarae ar y perdoneg – The girl is playing the piano. Y mae'r bachgen yn dringo'r wal – The boy is climbing the wall. Y mae yr asyn yn pori yn y cal – The donkey is grazing in the field. Direct method in language teaching, did you say? Here it was, in its infancy.

In history, we learned all the important dates – 55 BC, 1066, 1485, 1603, 1812, the heroes and prominent figures of the past; the genealogical tables of the kings and queens of England; the most important battles, Hastings, Agincourt, Crecy, Poitiers, Trafalgar and Waterloo. These lessons instilled in us a great feeling of pride in our country, and although we were sometimes inadequately fed and ill clad, we were all great patriots in those days.

In music, a chart called the modulator was placed on the blackboard which showed the scales in ascending order, doh, ray, me, fah, soh, la, te, doh. With the penchant of schoolboys for nicknames, we called them 'dough', 'rice', 'meat', 'fat', 'soap', 'lard', 'tea', 'dough'. We then sang the scales both up and down to get a rough idea of the tone of each note. Then the teacher would pick out notes at random from the chart. A few lessons of this kind soon familiarised us with the tone of each note. Then the teacher would show some hand signals for each note with which all music teachers are familiar. We would then run up and down the scales following the teacher's hand signals after which we would sing notes picked out at random. One day, we were practising this kind of performance when, to our surprise and delight, we found that we were singing the Welsh National Anthem 'Mae hen wlad fy nhadau'. In succeeding lessons we sang many songs in the same manner. We had become experts in sol-fa.

The last lesson Friday afternoon was usually devoted to an additional spelling lesson in which the teacher would write on the blackboard tricky and difficult words like rough, touch, sign, dough, believe, receive. He would give us about 15 minutes to memorise these and then he would ask individual pupils to spell one of the words. A weekly exercise of this type proved a great help to the weaker pupils.

By this time, I had obtained the reputation of being knowledgeable and of never being wrong. But, on one occasion, this led to utter disaster! We were having a lesson on animals and I mentioned an animal, which I called a 'waterus'. The teacher, knowing my reputation and fearing that there might be a slight gap in his knowledge, hurried to the next room to consult a teacher there. On looking through the glass partition, which separated the two rooms, I could see the teachers in earnest discussion with Mr Gomer Evans who finally shook his head. You will recall that Mr Evans taught in the hall, which also housed the headmaster's desk. The headmaster, on hearing the subject under discussion, came down to our room, curiosity aroused. He was anxious to know the story of this mysterious animal of which no one had ever heard and

Shool Hall showing size of class in 1913

which came from an usually reliable source. By this time, I had become thoroughly alarmed and wished I had kept a still mouth. The headmaster, on entering the room said, "Come on Ivor, describe this animal which is starting to disturb the whole school". I replied that it had a pair of tusks, sprouting whiskers and was called 'a waterus' because it lived mainly in the water. Revelation of the solution swept into the headmaster's mind: "You mean a walrus?" he exclaimed. "No," said I firmly, "waterus because it lives mainly in the water". But the headmaster, satisfied that he had found the solution to the mystery of this mythical animal was in no mood for further argument. He patted me encouragingly on the head, ruffled my hair in condolence at my defeat and left the room with a laugh. He left me thoroughly discomfited, but still unconvinced. Later, of course, I knew that I was wrong. Alas! I had lost my reputation of infallibility.

Modern day teachers complain if they have to teach classes of more than 30 pupils. I have at the present moment a class photograph taken in 1911 of my class Standard 2 with the teacher, Mr White, and the headmaster standing on each side of the group. This showed that the class contained 62 pupils. The last row contains boys slightly older and bigger than the rest. They were the boys who were kept back because they had not yet attained the standard of achievement required and there they stayed until they had. It seemed a very successful system.

One hears now of constant bullying in the schools, of some pupils being bullied to distraction. In some cases, boys are being driven to suicide, and cases of bullying are found among the girl pupils. I was only a little fellow but never in my school career can I recall being bullied. I became involved once when I was in Standard two in a fight with a boy called Willie Overton who set about me for no reason at all except for the fact that he was bigger than I was. He hurt me terribly, giving me a blow in the face, which split my lip. I fought back and I must have hurt him because he soon desisted. After that episode he troubled me no more, neither did anyone else. My reputation for retaliation must have got around. It reminded me later in life of the French tag: "Cet animal est tres mechant; quand on l'attaque il se defend". "This animal is very nasty; when attacked, he retaliates".

Boys have always fought one another and always will. But in our day they always fought fair, with fists and one against one. One reads nowadays of gangs of boys and sometimes girls hounding

Aberllechau Mixed School 1913

another boy, felling him to the ground and kicking him mercilessly, resulting in sometimes-fatal injuries. It makes one wonder when this all started and who started it.

In September 1915 we began the year in the new school building. To our eyes, accustomed to the cramped surroundings in the old school, it seemed an immense edifice, with an extensive assembly hall, large classrooms with new furniture and a huge playground. The assembly hall could now be used solely for the purpose for which it was intended; morning prayers and other school functions. The headmaster now had his own private room away from the assembly hall.

While we awaited the arrival of the headmaster to take prayers, we were ordered to chant the multiplication table 1 to 12. Sometimes we were lucky, as he came early and stopped us half way. At other times, we were not so lucky, when he arrived late after we had finished and we had to start all over again. It was all very boring, but at the end of our school days, we certainly knew our tables.

Another new development met our eyes when we entered the new school. Being accustomed to learning in a boys' school, we were surprised and somewhat horrified to discover that henceforward we were to have the company of strange beings called girls, whom hitherto I had viewed with a distant unseeing eye. I must confess that at first we found their unaccustomed presence rather overwhelming. I suspect that they felt the same way about us, for at times we found them gazing at us with curiosity.

The year passed uneventfully, as I was busy preparing for the entrance examination for the Grammar School. I was the sole candidate from our school and was successful in winning a scholarship. I entered the Porth County School for Boys in September 1916. A completely new life and a new world was there for me!

The school had been opened in 1896 as a result of the Welsh Intermediate Act of 1889. Originally it had been 'mixed' with boys and girls taught together but three years before my arrival the girls had left for a new adjacent school. The purpose of these Intermediate Schools was to prepare pupils for entry to universities and higher education which they did with great success. They came directly under the authority of the County Councils and were commonly known as 'County Schools'. Porth County School provided thirty free scholarships for Rhondda and Tonyrefail. Remaining available places were taken by those who had done well enough in the special entrance examination and whose parents were prepared to pay an annual fee of two pound plus cost of books.

Here in the sixth form, at the age of seventeen, I won a Rhondda University Scholarship of forty pounds a year, a Glamorgan County

Scholarship of sixty pounds a year, a Arthur Hopkins Memorial Scholarship of fifteen pounds a year, a Price Davies Scholarship of thirty pounds a year. I was not allowed to hold both a Rhondda Scholarship and a County Scholarship and had to give up the former. In all I was able to keep scholarships worth one hundred and five pounds a year with all fees paid. Here was financial independence, recognition of hard work and ability, the opportunity for success in a new open world.

Ivor Howells, back row, third from left, when he returned to Porth County as a member of staff.

Photographs provided by David carpenter

Britannia Hotel

Britannia 1910, Porth with Public House - Imperial Hotel

Pontypridd Road 1910

Hannah Street with a variety of gas lamps

William Evans of Corona first came to Porth to manage Peglers' grocery shop

Hannah Street, Porth

Station Street, Porth

Porth Dentist's Surgery above the shop, with promise of painless extraction

Station at the end of street

Porth Railway Station, 1900

Tramcars at the depot

Porth Street, Porth with Magistrates' Court on the right, and Cymmer Hill in the background

Porth Cottage Hospital with doctor's horse and trap

Porth County School 1900 with girls' entrance on the left

Porth County School with boys' entrance on the right

Porth County School staff 1946
Ivor Howells 2nd from top left